A PLACE TO REST

Poetry of Peace and Hope

Patrick Kavanagh

Amazon

To Tina
For keeping me alive when things got rough.
And for all the lovely people who have
supported me over the years.

CONTENTS

FOREWORD

In these pages I will be sharing poems with you that helped me through difficult times. They are musings and inspirations which I believe came from some sort of higher self to help me when I felt like giving up. I have also sprinkled the pages with some light-hearted poems , and I hope they make you laugh as much as they did me when they popped into my head.

Patrick W Kavanagh
09/04/2024

INTRODUCTION

I started to write poetry in 2010, after the passing of my late wife, Francis. I found that expressing my grief helped to create a network of people who gave mutual support to each other. I published eight books of poetry, mysticism, the fairies and dealing with grief, between then and 2019.

I became too ill to work in 2020, and came home to Ireland to go back to college. Due to a unexpected complications, my wife and I ended up homeless for over two years. We slept in our van for the nine months and were given temporary accomodation after I became seriously ill.

Finally, by 2024, my health had improved and we found a lovely apartment on the outskirts of Dublin.
These poems are my reflections on life, death and spirituality that kept me going through those difficult days.

CHAPTER 1: THE DAY BEFORE

Once upon a time my name was Hope, or Tolerance, or Love.
But in those days, I had no words for who I was or what I felt.
Once upon a time, my being was made from possibilities, potentialities and light.
But then, the words you taught me, showed me how to limit life.

Once upon a time, I knew of everything that never needed to be named.
Before the words you taught me, split my world into a million pieces that I could not join again.
Before the hammer of your wisdom smashed my world into a million words - my soul into a million shards.
Now I chase the scattered pieces of my soul into the ever-growing universe, while thinking that some 'Other' deals the cards.

But a wisdom, deeper than the world, is saying "Just be still".
I sit, or stand, or walk in stillness, and I let the world do as it will.
Flowing in and out with every breath, and every pause, and every step.
And in that stillness, both the world and I are one – but then they always were,
And I am just remembering who I was, the day before the day that I was born.

My Mother Once Told Me

"My mother once told me that fine words butter no parsnips.
I believed that the right words at the right time – if spoken well,
Could change the world.
But then, I believed in magic, and I still do."

I am still that child who wants to change the world into a better place.
Though you mightn't see it past the wrinkles on my face.
My greying hair conceals the fiery redness of my youth.
But deep inside a fire still burns for love, and light, and truth.

I am not an 'Urban Terrorist – unarmed',
Not like a teacher friend whose life was side-lined for a single march against the bomb.
A march where not a single soul, except the protestors, was harmed.
An educated man who could not get a job – who had to use his wits to get along.

I am not a hero nor a heroine – not like my dearest mentor, Anne.
She turned her deepest loss into a deep desire to help the world.
She touched so many lives, and helped me to discover who I really am.
She lived a life whose actions spoke much louder than her words.

Then there was Conn, who taught me that the simplest wisdom was the best.
That simple words and common sense was all we needed to

survive.

He was right, but simple words could not describe the dreams that broke my rest.

I could not find the simple words I needed to describe the many ways in which a world might thrive.

On resurrection day, I'll raise a glass to all my dear departed friends.

The curse of growing old is letting go of all those people that we loved, and all those happy days.

I live in hope that sometime, somewhere, somehow, we will meet again.

But until that day, I'll try to speak the truth that burns inside, a thousand different ways.

We Will Rise.

We may rise just like the eagle who commands the clear blue skies.
We may rise just like the sparrow as the eagle's shadow falls across his frightened eyes.
We may rise just like the morning sun to cast our light on all with eyes to see.
But we will rise to face each bright new day and be the best that we can be.

We may fall a thousand times each gifted, sacred day.
We may fail to see the wonder and the magic as we stumble on our way.
WE may fill each night with bitter tears and useless longing for the half-forgotten years.
But we will rise again each morning as we face once more our sadness and our fears.

We are stronger than the sharpest swords which heroes forged, when evil came with fangs and claws.
We are wiser than the sages and the wisest princes who pronounced our ancient sacred laws.
We are brighter than the sun, which soon enough will cool, but even now cannot outshine our spirit's vast eternal light.
Our dreams are softer and more gentle than the wistful moon which guides the traveller through this fleeting night.

We will rise one day to see that there never really was an 'us and them' or 'you and me.'

We will rise one day and realise that we already are the people whom we always wished to be.

We will rise to see acceptance eases every wound and kindness brings us every worthwhile answer to be found.

We will rise and build a world of peace and fairness where each creature whispers words of love with many different sounds.

The Endless Song

The Mother of the universe can never talk to you in words.
She has poured her life into the smallest spaces; spreading out into the world.
Creating life within the vast, expanding void that never ends.
She is much too small for human eyes to see, and much too large for human minds to comprehend.

Do not be offended that I call her 'Mother'.
The image that you place on her is just a measure of your faith.
But I have looked out on the earth and only mothers bring the earth to life.
And we who cannot see our mother stand like self-named orphans at her gate.

We can hear her in the songs of birds and in the wind.
We can hear her in the chimes we make that jangle in the breeze.
We can hear her in our hearts, but only if our hearts are true and bright
The smaller heart; the lesser chime; the smaller is our light.

All that lives can be her voice, and all who hear may sing her song.
It is the music of the universe; the gentle harmonies that guided life along.
Its sound created patterns that the world could follow into being.
It is the source of all that's heard, and all that's felt, and seen.

Buddha, Marx and Solomon

For all we know, there may be nothing new under the sun.
The world may be a clockwork toy that's slowly winding down.
There may have been a changeless plan for each and everyone.
As a God-child wound the clockwork universe and history was
first begun.

But if you search your heart, and look beneath your doubts and
all the lies,
You will hear that song which reaches out beyond the clouded
skies.
You will find a hope that neither misery nor doubt can ever quite
erase.
You will touch that spark you share with all of life – a spark that
led you past your darkest days.

Some will call the spark their Goddess, some will see it as the
One of Ancient Days.
It matters little – we are merely story-tellers; - lost in all our
strange and simple ways.
Though we seem to be divided, - when we touch that spark, we
know that we are one.
As we always were, despite our many different tales, -
For truly, there is nothing new beneath the sun.

Dispossessed

I haven't had a country since I learned how many people countries have enslaved.
I haven't had a country since I saw the never-ending rows of young men's graves.
I haven't had a country since I watched my comrades drunk and drowning in their tears.
Singing songs of hate, my country taught them in their young and foolish years.

I haven't had religion since the day I realised that my religion lied.
Religion picked my pocket while it kept me occupied with staring at the skies.
I haven't had religion since they found the children lying in an unmarked grave.
Religion without love was just a club to hide the broken lives, and all misery they'd made.

I haven't had a final truth since I discovered every truth is, in some measure, flawed.
So many people see so many different truths, - so many people worship different gods.
To bomb a planet into righteousness, to me, - seems quite insane.
A million dead can't change their minds, and in a hundred years, you'll change your mind again.

The stories that they told a thousand years ago are no more sacred than the stories that they tell today.

The only truth is who you love, and who you help, and who you smile at every day.

Suffering is real, and only suffering can soften hearts and help us understand,

That if we walk this world as exiles, we can look within each other's hearts to find the promised land.

Twilight

How do you feel when doubts and lack of pride slip secretly into your world?

What happens when the walls that once protected your beliefs begin to crack?

When tiny sparks from distant stars and galaxies slip past the filters of your mind.

The beauty lifts your spirits, yet you ache for all the worlds you left behind.

Self-delusion waited all your life to be the first of many veils to fall.

Your shame, and guilt and anger quickly fade away. Your life was just a story, – after all!

And as your many idols crack and crumble, – as your mind allows your spirit to be free,

You realise you only played a part, - that you became the person you were always meant to be.

Yet, nothing ever done was wasted – nothing ever done will cease to be.

The beauty and the pain that you created ripple out into eternity.

You have changed the world forever- thanks to you the world will never be the same.

So, it matters little if you sleep forever, or if you return again.

A Coin for the Ferryman

In the end, Death is king and he comes for his dues.
But life was his gift, and there's nothing to lose.
Like a two-headed coin that was tossed at our birth,
A random pronouncement of status and worth.

Sometimes he comes as we sleep in our beds.
While dreams of a new life slip into our heads.
He waits like a shadow, in dark, worn-out robes.
To free us from all of our toils and our woes.

I know him as silence – a dark, empty void.
A place of repose, down a long winding road.
If our journey is long, - we are ready to rest.
We have already given our blood and our best.

If the journey is short, - then the tears won't be ours.
We leave sorrow behind and the long lonely hours.
For those who have loved us, and can't understand
a god who kills children – with blood on his hands.

Death may come with a missile at insane expense,
From countries where citizens starve on the street.
Where patriots cheer with no soles on their shoes,
and they think it's a victory each time that they lose.

Death may come from a tyrant – a man who's deranged.
Who rides his horse naked in snow and in rain.
Death may come from a weakling, who's long sold his soul,

To accumulate wealth when he's feeble and old.

But Death will come stalking the good and the bad.
Their only reward is the lives that they had.
Lives which may live forever beyond earthly time.
Repeating the memories of kindness or crime.

Toxic Masculinity

I used to love Doc Peterson, – when he was just a stand-up guy.
I watched his lectures on the psyche, – on all the who's and where's and why's.
A pinch of Jung, a splash of Freud – he really knew his stuff.
I gobbled up his wisdom, and I couldn't get enough.

I understood his stance on pronouns, - though I didn't quite agree.
I have no problem letting you be you, - or 'They' be 'He' or 'She'.
If you tell me that your name is Fred, or Freda, - I am happy to agree.
I know my world will be a better place, – if you let me be me.

And when he speaks of gender roles, I really feel his pain.
So many people pray to see the good old days come back again.
But this big old world is changing, and that may come as a surprise,
If we are busy looking to the past, with biased, blinkered eyes.

We don't need men who sire 100 children – just to send them off to war.
Or men who cannot understand compassion, - men who do not know what love is for.
A brand-new world needs brand-new people who can keep an open mind.
It's time to build a better world for all of us, and leave the past behind.

Tears.

I think my tears are falling for the lives I never lived.
The doors I never opened and the gifts I never gave.
I think I cry for all the hopes that never were fulfilled.
The dreams that never could come true, -
The dreams that never will.

I think my tears are falling for the children who could never have a life.
I cry for all the children who grew up to face a world that never seemed to care.
The children who were lost before their lives could blossom into joy.
The children who survived to live a haunted, loveless life,
And never understood the reason why.

I think my tears are falling for the ones whose lives are made of memories,
So many friends who briefly shone, - then faded into silence much too soon.
I cry for all the friends I'll never see again, because I lived too long.
But then, perhaps my tears may someday end,
Perhaps, someday, I'll learn to sing a brand-new song?

I wonder why my tears are falling, - if I even cry for me.
My tears have mostly been for what the world became – for what the world could be.

I tried to write a brand-new story, - but I guess I don't know how.
I live in gratitude for what has been the luckiest of lives...
And yet I find my tears are falling now.

If My Words Had Wings

If my words had wings, I'd cast them to the sky.

If my words had wisdom, they could tell us all the reasons why.

If my words were simple, they could help the children understand,

How this world of beauty brought us so much sadness.

Are the gods to blame, or is it just the fault of Man?

If our eyes were not so blind, we'd see the beauty that we've left behind.

If our eyes could see more clearly, think of all the wonders we would find.

If our eyes were open, we would not mistake our darkness for the night.

We'd no longer stumble with our eyelids tightly closed,

We could end our slavery to darkness; We could find our freedom in the light.

If our ears could listen, we would hear the sacred music of the spheres.

We could hear the heartbeat of the earth – were we not deafened by the noisy years.

We could learn the wisdom of the ancients – but we never can be still.

No one sits and listens to our elders or our ancestors.

And maybe, no one ever will?

Our heads will be forever in the clouds until we learn to touch the earth.

Very few can understand the value of a single patch of dirt.
Very few remember, Mother Earth still feeds us,
And her strength is in the air, the water and the soil.
Every effort that we make is wasted when it's not for Mother Earth for whom we toil.

I Believe in you.

I believe in you, no matter what the world may say.

I have seen your light outshine your darkness, almost every single day.

I have dreamed your dreams, and held your hand each time we glimpsed the other side.

That place where dreams are written, and the place where darkness cannot hide.

Every one of us must live a story that the world has told us long before our world was born.

A story that was written in our hearts, and in our loves and in our songs.

A story that we rarely get to question, 'til we reached the point of no return.

But still, before the final act, we sometimes see the script; we choose our path; we watch our old, out-dated, story burn.

I believe in you. You gave me hope when all my hope was gone.

It was you who taught me how to see the world anew; to write a brand-new song.

All of us are lost within a story, and we rarely get to understand the reason why.

I was lost in grief until an angel took my hand and raised my vision to the sky.

Stars.

Have you ever wondered about all those bright lights in the sky? Many of us cannot tell if they are stars or planets, but that matters little.

Maybe, we should take their stories away from those who have only given them numbers.

They deserve better than that – don't they?

Maybe we should name them after all the children we have lost?

Tell the brief stories of their lives each day, so that we survivors can learn to be kind.

But many of their stories will never be known.

Not the ones who died along with their families in so many places.

Places like Bangladesh; Darfur; Rwanda; Armenia; Circassia; Cambodia; Holodomor; Germany; China; Eurasia; Turtle Island; South America, and Gaza.

And for all those millions of children who will never be known, - Who will never have a life -

Perhaps we can ask the stars when the bloodshed will end…

The Age of Myth

Beyond the realm of judgement, there's a world where all the past; the present; and the future lies.

It is world of countless oceans; endless seas; - of mystic mountains and of endless skies.

You and I may sit around a campfire, as we tell the many tales that made the story of our lives.

The Age of Myth has many mansions and things we loved and lost will be our guides.

Don't be fooled by time. What seem like memories will live forever – if we choose.

Some of us are drawn to battle; Some are lovers; some of us were even born to sing the blues.

Even 'ordinary' lives, are lives beyond comparison, – are lives beyond compare.

Every one of us has gazed upon the void to name the gods and angels who await us there.

Some of us may choose a life within a universe which seems like nothing more that just a clockwork toy.

Some of us may choose a goddess, or a god of love, - or seek a life in payment for a life – and eye in payment for an eye.

Be careful what you wish for – each of us can hold a universe within our minds; - A world within our hands.

If we are fragments of an Ancient God – the Age of Myth awaits our expectations and commands.

I am not a god-abiding creature. Every God I knew has blessed me and then sent me on my way.

I chose the path of kindness only when the path of war had cut too deep; When war had nothing left to say.

I would choose the path of Wisdom, but my tiny cup could never hold the ocean of Her dreams.

So, I wander as a fool who tries to peer beyond the veil of lies – beyond a life where nothing's as it seems.

Just Another Poem that Rhymes

Is it still a poem, that has no tears or blood upon the page?
Is it still a poem without some words of anguish or of rage?
I can't write these modern poems – the streams of consciousness
That pour out unrelenting pain or angst without a single break,
My words just end up rhyming - no matter what approach I choose to take.

When we think about it, there is plenty in our lives that we could rant about.
All the stuff we didn't want' and all the stuff we had to do without.
Maybe, if I didn't rhyme – I'd squeeze in all the stuff that doesn't fit?
Halitosis, alopecia, haemorrhoids and dandruff - spots and pimples, too,
I could talk about the challenges that other poets never do.

I was thinking – birth is just a miracle, and death's our final chance to shine.
Unless we're Stalin, - folks will gather, and convince each other that we did just fine.
I thought that life was just a battle-ground. It took a lifetime for my thoughts to shift.
And now, a thousand poems into my repertoire,
I realise, that life – for all its faults is just the greatest gift.

But that doesn't leave you much to say. It's pretty dull to write that life's okay.

I think that we all need a touch of drama spicing up our day.

We learn what's up by looking down – we recognise our smiles when they replace a frown.

And in a world where every love will one day lead to loss, we learn to value every precious day.

We learn to live in gratitude for everything we have that, soon enough, will fade away.

CHAPTER 2:   BE GENTLE

Be gentle with your heart,
The world can change within a single beat.
Tread lightly in the world,
And treat with kindness, all the people you may meet.

Wisdom costs us dearly,
The price that we must pay, - we pay in sorrow and in loss.
And all the times we try, - we ask ourselves the reason why,
But still, we carry on the burden of survival, for the sake of those
we love.
And gaze in silent question at the grey and sullen sky.

Rage against the storms that carry all we love away.
Turn your back against the setting sun that leaves us cold, or
hungry or alone at end of day.
Shake your fist and cry out to the moon, - howling out with
sorrow like the solitary wolf.
Touch the earth with dewy tears as sunrise makes us face
another day.
But still the earth will turn, and we will heal, - for that is nature's
way.

Children

Wisdom spreads itself across the vast expanse we call the universe. A universe which may not reach an end.
Love existed since before the dawn of time and stretches to a future we can never comprehend.
We dip our tiny chalices into the deep and endless sea that flows from timeless voids into infinity.
And yet, we think we know the one true name of God – and even claim to know who He, or She, may be.

Our tiny cups can't even hold the smallest dregs of knowledge.
Our eyes are blind to but a tiny spectrum of the light.
Yet we dare to stand upon the mountain top and claim to know what's wrong and what is right.
We know there is a better way to be, and those who filled their tiny cups with love have shown the way.
But remember that the way is just a path, a pointer, and a finger pointing where our destination lays.

We are children playing in the sand. But we are not alone.
Reaching out – we'll find that Love will take our hand.
We have much to learn, and much to do, and we must grow a little more – before we reach the promised land.
We cannot go there if our hands are soaked in blood. We cannot go there when our hearts are filled with hate.
We cannot pass beyond the troubled world we see and leave behind the hungry children at our gate.

Jealous Gods.

It's a gift that few possess.
To wake up soaked with dew beneath a harvest moon.
To hear the angels whisper in the wind.
To lay among the meadow flowers.
To hear the heartbeat of the planet in the silent hours.

You may call it madness.
To touch a tree and feel the rising sap in Spring.
To feel the warm caress of spirits in the Summer's wind.
To lay upon the Autumn's fallen leaves.
To kiss the icy Earth and feel the Winter's peace.

My grandad had the gift, or so they say.
Luckily for me, he sanctified his wife.
Blessing her with vibrant, pregnant life.
Before they dragged him from his marriage bed.
Before they chained him to a workhouse cot, instead.

He could cure the dropsy and the warts.
But sometimes he forgot the 'proper' prayers.
He told the future and the secrets of the past.
But as his godless, churchless, congregation grew,
The clergy of another god demanded of him, what they felt was
due.

They cleansed his tongue with red-hot crosses.
After that, he could no longer speak.
They beat the evil spirits from his body.

Left him broken. Trapped in silence. Soaked in blood and snot.
Forever silenced. On his filthy workhouse cot.

They say it is a gift that few possess.
They say it is a grace to hear the angels sing.
They say that just a few can hear the voices of the gods.
But choose your company. Be wary of your fold.
Before you name the gods of old.

LIFE

My own little place.
A moment of grace.
My time in the sun.
My journey is done.

The smiles and the tears.
The long lonely years.
Someone by my side.
Then happiness dies.

The greeting of friends.
All comrades attend.
Will we meet again,
When everything ends?

Our enemies too,
Must be given their due.
Our anger prevails,
When everything fails.

We fight for our love.
Our love longs to fight.
We fight to escape,
That long endless night.

Our story completed.
The stage lights go down.
I hope that we leave with a smile -

Not a frown.

Why Am I?

I woke last night because I had a dream that we were going back to war.

Something deep inside recoiled in horror; War is not what we are for.

I was a soldier once, but now I'm much too old to face the bombs and bullets,

Yet they'll find me soon enough inside my bombed-out lair.

Like the wounded and the children, I'll be blotted from existence,

By a lunatic with medals on their chest who never learned to love,

who never learned to care.

We are crying out for answers, and protection from the ones who think they know.

Who will save us from the vengeful gods who cast the orphans out on Christmas eve to perish in the snow?

Who will save us from the men of greed who know no god but gold, and grind us down like wheat –

The well-fed men in limousines whose drivers take them past us as we lie here on the streets?

Who will save us from the waves of brave young men who learn to fight before they ever learn what life is for?

Before they ever learn to hold their babies in their arms, they rush through Hell's wide-open door.

While poets cry, and mothers wonder why they die, and what it is they're fighting for?

Rags and Feathers.

Rags and feathers are the way the children born of love will fly today.

We drag our tattered wings of wax and wishes up beyond the travelled way.

On mountaintops and high-rise blocks, we brace our wings against the breeze.

To fly, or fall, becomes our only prayer, - we cannot live our lives on bended knees.

We are children once again, - born once more in ignorance and awe.

We cannot cling to hate or pain when every dream they sold us has been flawed.

Wood and bone, and rags and feathers are our teachers now.

We know, that in the fantasies we weave, the truth will shine, somehow.

Are we certain? We are only certain that this moment is the one that slips away.

This moment is the only chance we have to laugh, to love, to play.

This moment is the pinnacle of truth, this moment is the purpose of our youth.

This moment is the life we have which quickly fades away.

The sun begins to rise as rags and feathers ruffle in the breeze.

The golden glow of morning forms a web of light across the rooftops and the trees.

Will our hopes be dashed upon the ground or lift us far beyond despondence and unease?

It matters little if we fly or fall, - for there is nothing left within our hearts but peace.

Dublin Burning.

Let's burn our way back to the times of poverty and hate.

Why would anyone want peace and comfort, anyway?

We can wake each morning to the smell of burning cars and buses,

At the start of each new hate-filled, empty day.

Let's go and tear down all the meaning in our lives.

Who wants peace and liberty and who needs human rights?

Why not let our lives be smashed by fear and mindless hate,

Rather than to live in peace and welcome strangers at our Gate.

We can die in hovels or in trenches like we did in World War one.

We've had peace for far too long – let's start another one!

We can live like rats in bombed out building while we tear our children's world apart.

Burn the world back to the stone age – let the roaches make a fresh new start.

Freedom

In the end, we all let go.
Our cares and worries lie like autumn leaves beneath the winter's snow.
With, perhaps, one final sigh,
We say goodbye to all our sorrows and our questions why?
We finally lie still and peaceful underneath a winter sky,

Our whirling, fretful wonderings are blown away by wind and time,
Finally, we say goodbye to all the reasons and the rhymes,
Our thoughts are blown away like autumn leaves,
And there is nothing left but peace,
As we lay calm and still like fallen leaves.

Perhaps the sky becomes our final friend?
Our ashes, flying in the wind, are scattered far and wide.
Captured by the wind, they fly to freedom.
Loneliness no longer cramps our style, and we become the Earth again.
Perhaps forever? Or perhaps for just a little while…

Dreamtime

The dreaming time has come at last and we can let our burdens go.
Autumn lays her leafy blanket on our shoulders as we gently drift away.
Winter may soon hide our sleeping forms beneath her soft white snow.
But now it is the time when dreams and memories must hold us in their sway.

Never think your dreams are wasted moments. Many dreams have changed the world.
Wisdom can be found in all those memories we thought we'd left behind.
Drifting back into the forest of our minds like leaves that drift and twirl,
We wander ancient paths and gaze at fallen leaves to see what we may find.

We trace each vein with childish awe on golden leaves we cup within our palms.
The forest smell that we once knew so well assails our senses as we walk through leafy piles.
Wandering here among the autumn forests on the paths that soon may lead us home,
We may find a wisdom far beyond the world's misleading and unfriendly wiles.

Stories

Stories are the ancient forge in which our dreams were formed.
Our mothers whispered tales into our wombs before we ever knew the light.
Floating. Safe within a living sea which built our sinews and our bones.
Our mothers told us all that we would be in gentle, loving tones.

Without our stories there would be no past, no future – just a fleeting glimpse of now.
The world would slip away before our thoughtless eyes and fade without a trace.
No one would be wise enough to tell us who to be, or when, or where, or how.
There would be no courage, no companionship, no magic and no grace.

The flowers would never have a name and roses would not be the bloom of love.
The stars would spring to life unheeded and be unremembered when they die.
There would be no lovers gazing up in wonder at the beauty of a moonlit sky.
There would be no poets dreaming of the reasons why we live and why we die.

Maybe there's a Heaven?

I hope that there's a heaven where the children can be free.
But maybe it's a heaven for a better world than this.
A world where children don't learn hatred on their father's knee.
When I think of all those barbed wire fences stretching out into
eternity,
It's not the kind of heaven where I think I want to be.

Maybe there's a heaven that is meant for everyone who leaves
their hate behind.
A heaven I could live in without pushing thoughts of dying
children from my mind.
A heaven where the children can be safe from poverty and need,
A heaven where we have no need for bigotry or greed.
You see, I'm old and running out of time and that's the kind of
heaven that I need.

If I can't find that kind of heaven then I may as well choose hell.
At least I'll be with folk like me who tried their best, but fell.
I'll walk there with the children who were born unwanted and
unblessed.
I'll walk there with the outliers, the infidels and atheists when
it's my time to rest.
I am not wise, nor pure enough to please a god who puts his
children to such fearful tests.

Gifting the Moon

How I wish that it had been within my power to give to you the moon.

That radiant light that beautifies the starry night but fades away so soon.

Moving gently through her quarters. Growing 'til her beauty fills the sky.

But it was not within my power to gift to you the moon, - or even tell you why.

That was long ago, but I still gaze up at that glowing orb that lights the sky.

My childish dreams of you and me weren't meant to be, and there were many reasons why.

But you were my hope and all my dreams. You were the life I fought so hard to live.

But I was just a child as well, and though I tried, - it's me I can't forgive.

Death refused me, so, I tried in many, different ways to find some comfort in my loss.

Acceptance brought some peace, but, deep inside, my heart was tethered to the past.

I was given so much love by others, but I'd lost the other loves for which I craved.

I was torn between two worlds and could not see a way to bridge that rift I'd made.

You were my angels and you taught me how to leave the past

behind and learn to love.

My wounded heart had finally begun to heal, and you became the centre of my world.

When that world was shattered, I was blinded by despair. I fooled myself that you were doing fine.

Now I only wish that I had fought much harder for the life that, long ago, could have been yours and mine.

CHAPTER 3: MEMORIES OF DUBLIN

Stephen's Green was such a joy, when I was little more than just
a boy,
Where pretty girls with long dark curls sat soaking up our
fleeting summer Sun.
On Grafton Street, I'd stop and listen to the buskers, as the world
passed slowly by,
Then wander down the cobbles to the green - my business in the
city almost done.

There was still the 'Dandelion' to see – a market with a hundred
tiny stalls,
Once a thriving mill, its wheels had long stood still, - but still
there was a penny to be made.
A thousand shoppers searched for bargains in her narrow,
rough-stone halls.
But now it's gone, the world's moved on, and in its place, we have
a glass arcade.

Near the Ha'penny bridge, along the Liffey walks, the buses lined
the stone-walled quay,
The bookshops and the coffee shops combined, with tired old
books on battered shelves,
I'd often stop to rest and take the view, and buy a cup of tea,
Then delve into those well-worn books and fill my mind for free.

Moore Street, with her makeshift wooden stalls and old

converted prams,

The raucous cries of women selling fruit and clothes and jams.

Their voices ringing loud and clear, "Get your oranges and pears! Get your apples here!"

And though they are a long-lost memory, my mind still hears them now across the years.

You'll always be my Dublin, even if I live a thousand miles away.

The rancid smell of Liffey's mud may fill the air, but you will always be my one true love, - my city fair,

My mind is never far from Dublin docks where seagulls screech and play,

No matter where I live, my spirit walks your grimy streets, - my heart is always there.

Trusting Life.

It starts so early, none of us can name the moment or the day.

None of us can tell the moment when our trust in life began to slip away.

Waking in the middle of the night, - no hugs, no warmth, no soothing light.

Loving parents fast asleep and unaware we lie in sodden nappies, - stiff with fright.

So many parents frightened to allow our fragile bodies sleep beside them in their bed,

And so, we lie awake, abandoned, in our pretty cots with lonely thoughts arising in our heads.

A little older, and we know the names of all the creatures that surround our busy day.

But who knows the names of all the terrors who are hiding underneath our beds, when day has gone away?

Our instincts still live in a world where death is just a movement in the undergrowth away.

Our beds are much too low. There is no sleeping adult close enough to keep the fear away.

No one seems to understand the ancient and primeval thoughts that hold our minds in sway,

And when we cry, the kindest parents smile, and maybe hug, then brush our tears, our fears, and all our trust, away.

We ask our parents about sex, or Santa-Klaus and many of them only tell us lies.

They bluff and bluster; - but we're children – we can see the falsehood in their eyes.

We go to school, - they talk of love, but bully us until we see the world the way they want the world to be.

We grow up learning how to hide the secret things we know in case somebody else can see.

To tell our parents of our doubts would break their fragile hearts, so silence soon becomes our only friend.

And by the time that we are old enough to speak, our silence – and our lives have almost reached the end.

We learn to trust our death the way we never really learned to trust our lives.

Our death can never be denied. It rises like a ragged spectre, just before our very eyes.

But silence hugs us closely – just as silence always had, through all those busy years.

For we would spare our children's fragile hearts from all our broken dreams and all our fears.

Then as the shadows of our fading minds fly back across the wondrous stories of our lives – that cinema of fate and blood and time.

We realise, the Universe had always held our hand, and everything, - despite our tears, had always worked out fine.

We Are History

Our memories, since birth are fleeting, ghost-like, fragile things.
Our histories contain the briefest stories of the rise of emperors and kings.
The moment of our birth, though filled with overwhelming light and sound and pain,
is lost in time.
The moment's passed and, though we wrack our brains and search our dreams, will not come back again.

And yet we knew our mother's voice, - we knew the place where we could rest.
Our searching lips sought comfort from her soft and waiting breasts.
We merged into this waiting world as if our introduction to its denizens had been already made.
As if the gods had written on our hearts – the names of all the creatures we must cherish - and the ones we must evade.

This world was ours before we ever touched the earth or gazed up at the skies.
We slipped into its rough embrace before we knew our name and race.
And though our strange and restless brains had brought us far beyond the range of Eden's gentle rains,
We stole her fire and burned her world – and set out with our blazing torches to remake her world again.

We are history. We write the past and plan the future while the present moment slips away.

We learn the things we do not need to know, and sleepwalk through our ever-busy days.

And though the blueprint of our lives was written in the stars long passed, and ancient oceans flow through every vein.

We blunder, thinking we are orphans, through a fleeting world that may not come again.

Silence

Beyond our first goodbye, or maybe, just before our last hello.
They say there is a world where only fools and madmen go.
A world which lies between the ticking of each second, on this clockwork world we see.
A world where you're no longer 'You', and I'm no longer 'Me'.

Perhaps we are each other in this world beyond/beneath/between the skies?
Perhaps the silence that it brings is just the absence of our dreams and lies?
Perhaps there is no need to dream when we are all who make all dreams come true?
And yet we must return to face a fleeting world which never tells us what it is, that we must do.

The silence deep inside us wants to take the world and hold it safely in our arms.
The silence looks into the other and it sees the child inside with all its flaws and charms.
To the silence, life and death are equal – yet it yearns to fill the world with love.
Our clockwork minds can't understand. We build our tower of Babel and we look for wisdom up above.

Sometimes, I want to live forever, but my clockwork life's already running down.

I want to leave my mark upon the world, but who can say a poet's greater than a clown?

And long before I put a pen to paper, I have been a clown for many, many, years.

And maybe poetry is just a way for clowns to share their joys, their laughter and their tears?

The silence grows inside me, but I feel my race is not yet run.

So many things I want to do – so much I've not yet done.

May those who walk the lonely path beside me bear their scars and aches with pride.

The battle may be far from over, but my silence tells me we are on the winning side.

Never Broken.

I've always longed for truth and knowledge, but sometimes the truth is just so hard to see.
Our science has gone from babe to toddler, but there is so much to learn, - a greater science that's yet to be.
Our gods and goddesses bring little comfort to the many, - they can only touch those precious few, -
The outliers who were born into a hostile world already knowing without words, the things the world must do.

But the labyrinth of the mind is deep and dark, and many never find their way back home.
Their landlocked spirits gaze out at the endless sea, while restless feet are forced to roam.
Children of a different world of endless night, they struggle to adjust to garish light.
This world gives little comfort to their souls, and nothing seems to ever turn out right.

Changelings, friends and fellow travellers! – you were never broken. You were born into a broken world.
A world where evil took the reins and drives the kind and decent folk among us to the edge of dark despair.
But we have just to reach within to touch the magic and the love that's sleeping there,
We have only to remember what we knew when we were born to grasp the power, - for we are spirit's heirs.

We know the world we want. We know the world as it was

meant to be.

The myths and legends that divide us are the half-forgotten memories of how life used to be.

Long before they built their walls of mud, and later on, the walls within our minds,

As new-born gods we came into a bright new world to see what love born into flesh would find.

When Jennifer Met Mulligan

When Jennifer met Mulligan that night at Charlie's Keg,
The music was quite deafening; the pub was filled to brim.
She saw him past her empty glass, as he rose above the rim.
She had no eye for any other as she fixed her eye on him.

She knew right then the truth of it – as she hauled him from the
floor.
That Mulligan would be the one – the man that she'd adore.
He asked her if she'd like a pint – she helped him cross the floor.
And drunk with love, they pushed and shoved, - until they
reached the door.

They found their way into the snug, and snuggled up real tight.
She made him sit on her left side, as she couldn't see him on the
right.
He lay his leg behind his head – in case it might get stolen.
She gazed at him with her good eye, - her heart, with love was
swollen.

They'd found the half that makes a whole, and happiness was
theirs.
He read all those tiny labels, and she helped him up the stairs.
Like every happy couple they enhanced each other's flaws,
And bit their lips each time they had to sit with their in-laws.

No matter if we're rich or poor, or old, or young or gay.

Out there we'll find that perfect match to help us on our way.

Well, I'm sure they won't be perfect, - they'll be just like you and
I.

They'll fight and cuss, then love and laugh, and cuddle up and
sigh.

Talking to the Wind.

I will talk to the wind. When she blows harsh and stern I will shout in anger.

I will watch my words being torn and scattered, as she sends my angry words away.

When she is gentle and warm, I will whisper words of love and watch them drift into a sunny day,

Like the tiny windblown seeds, that in their time will grow, and flower, and fade away.

I will speak my wisdom and my folly to the trees, and I will not be turned away.

The trees already know my hopes and fears, they've heard a million times the things that I might say.

And if my love, the Wind will give them voice, the leaves will whisper softly in my ear.

And as I lay upon the forest floor, the gentle moss will wipe away my tears.

I will sing my songs where mighty rivers drown my voice against the stalwart stones.

The rivers do not need to hear my voice. The waters hurry on their way back home.

Home, where in the dark and lonely sea the life that lives in me was once begun.

The waters do not need to hear my voice. The Sea and I are one.

The Sea and I light up in wonder as we gaze up at the Moon and Stars.

Our sisters shine so bright and yet they seem a little lonely as they are so far away.

But in my heart and in my veins, I feel their touch. I feel the edges of the Universe that quickly speed away.

And yet, so many wiser men have said the Universe was born in just a single day.

I do not know these things. I only know the Universe and I are one.

I reach out to Her cold embrace and hear a million different songs.

I dance and sway within the rhythm of Her music and I call this dance my life.

Yet, what I call myself is just a tiny part of one immense, unending life.

Not Much Of A Guru.

He didn't seem much of a guru to me.
He needed a bath and he wanted some tea.
The café was rough, and I was alone,
A life-weary traveller who longed for their home.

I'd finished my meal, but I bought him another.
As rough as he looked, he was human – a brother.
We sat at a table, outside in the sun,
So, I lit up a cigarette – once he was done.

I lit him another – we gazed at the street, -
At all the strange people that I might yet meet.
"They are not very happy", he said with a smile.
"Do you often wonder if life is worthwhile?"

You should be just as happy, as a poor man like me,
Whose day can be blessed with a meal and some tea".
The smoke was a bonus – it made up my day.
I have only a question with which to repay".

"**I**f a poor man is happy – what more should we do?
Should we spare his poor feet with some nice sturdy shoes?
Would a nice long warm coat add more joy to the world?
And maybe a bath to look good to the world?"

"**P**erhaps you might teach him a trade or a skill?

And then he could work and could eat to his fill?
Somewhere safe for his rest from a long, hard day's toil?
And his life would have comfort - at least for a while."

"But to tell you the truth, I'm not long for this world.
And I'd never ask such from a strip of a girl.
But imagine the joy that the giving would bring,
In a world where a beggar could live like a king."

I walked back to my flat as I thought on his words.
I barely survived, - his appeal was absurd.
But what if the whole world could learn how to share?
And then, none of us needed to live with such cares?

Today, I Spoke to the Trees.

They had reached out to me, almost silently and without words.
I answered back in simple appreciation for their existence.
Neither they, nor I, tapped into the vast ocean of unconscious
knowing.
There was no conversation beyond the meeting of life with life.

I had gone to no sacred forests high on the mountain.
I had simply returned to my car and stood in the centre of their
almost silence.
There had been no meditation other than regaining control of a
disobedient heart.
And yet, I stood in the circle of distant trees and realised that Life
was enough.

It didn't matter if I lived for 66 years or 66 minutes.
If my life was short and full of misery, or long and full of joy.
Compared to the gift of life; – the sacredness of being,
The differences were much too small to measure.

On Being Enough.

I am enough. I know it, - yet sometimes I feel a yawning ache inside.

Where just an hour ago my heart was full of gratitude – I feel an aching void.

Suddenly, my words no longer rhyme, the world has lost a little shine.

And though, I know the dullness comes from me, - there is no easy antidote that I can see.

I could have a soothing drink? A whisky or the spirits of my choice to wash away the thoughts, I think.

So many pathways to oblivion, but none of them will last. The feelings will return when nothingness has passed.

I feel too tired to walk this mood away, the wind's too cold – the night's too wet.

I turn the TV on, but nothing grips my mind or helps me to forget.

I pace at first, and then I brave the porch and light a cigarette.

I comb my mind but I can't even find exactly what it is I'm trying to forget.

The moon hangs low and bright between the clouds. The wind is whispering in the trees.

I listen carefully. Perhaps the wind brings comfort or advice from far away for me?

The wind blows harder as I lean down to the ashtray and I crush my cigarette.

It didn't help me anyway, to find the source of all the feelings that I try hard to forget.

I drank the wind and drew her deep into my lungs, and slowly I exhaled my pain away.

My peace returned, at least for just a while, until somehow, I find a better way.

PATRICKWILLIAMKAVANAGH

The King of the Faeries.

Sprite of foot and keen of eye,
With sombre beauty, I can scarce describe,
He never told the truth, but never really lied,
The music of his voice brought tears of longing to my eyes.

The labyrinth of his mind touched mine and made me weep,
for all the wishes that my long-lost childhood could not keep.
I stood amazed, entranced, but careful to maintain a steady glance,
My wishes were within my grasp, and yet, single blink might spoil my chance.

He bowed so low, he swept the ground,
his sparkling laughter echoed all around,
With promises of servitude, his smiling eyes belied,
he granted me my wishes with a gleaming, imp-like look within his eyes.

A moment's pause, I must remember ancient lore and wish with all my wiles.
"I wish for Health" ... and once again he gave that dreadful smile.
"Granted! You shall die as healthy as you are today, -
Now two more wishes, and I shall be on my way!"

I shuddered as the icy chill ran down my spine, and silently I wished we had not met.
But still, I had a chance to prosper here, for had I not still got two

wishes left.

"I wish myself a long and happy life!", again that awful smile that turned my heart to stone,

"One hundred years I add unto your span, and you shall live it happily, though you may live it hungry and alone".

I sighed, I cast my eyes down to the ground, - I knew I had but one last wish to turn my fate around.

"I wish, my Lord, that I had not been so bold, to try to draw upon your power,

I wish, my Lord, that I had not belaboured you at this late hour".

"I wish, my lord, to leave you and this sacred place as it was found".

He smiled again with warmth; my heart began to fill with joy.

"You had three wishes, but you added more and set me free,

Your kindly act has filled my ancient heart, once more, with childish glee.

I wish you well my friend, I wish you wealth and health and joy",

And, as he faded back into the mist, he waved a last goodbye.

A Web of Dreams

Our thoughts are like the finest spider webs the Universe can spin.
Spun by words from threads of nothingness to let the Universe begin.
Born of nothingness, she spun the thread that wove the tapestry of life.
The warp and weave, the joy and grief, the darkness and the light.
She spun the web of dreams that bring both sorrow and delight.

Have you seen them on a summer's morning, lit by sunlight on the dew?
A million spider-webs that stretch across the fields until they fade from view.
The distant mountains hold as many webs, but far beyond our feeble sight.
Just as we cannot see the webs of thought that spread across the universe into the endless night.
Each strand of every web a tiny spark of our Divine and endless light.

Your thoughts are not your own. Your thoughts are woven from the language that you speak.
How could you fight the words that shaped your mind when you were frail and small and weak?
The person who you think you are is just a shadow – woven from your parent's dreams.
And yet, it is a thing of beauty, in a universe where nothing's as

it seems.

A universe, where in the silence and the shadows, we are one with our eternal dreams.

Words of Power.

Despite my love of words, it seems to me that Silence holds the greater power.
She has been my teacher since before the spinning of this tiny globe we share.
She held the multitude of nameless patterns for the Universe before the Universe was born.
I call Her 'She' - for how can anything be borne of Man – except the things that lead us to despair?

But I have always loved my words, - the sound of them, the taste of them,
The texture of the consonants that touch the tongue as if in play
The slow and easy flow of vowels that ease the breath,
The soft vibration of their tones that, in our breathing out, will draw our stress away.

An example: "Home" … Spoken soft and low, - a mantra that will mean a lot to many.
Some will fill with tears of gratitude, or sorrow – some with tears of bitterness and pain.
For some it is a golden glow for others it is blue as bruises, red as blood or black as any stain.
Just a word, and yet it brings back memories of times we know will never come again.

But where exactly is our home? Is it the place where we were born or is it where we lay our head?
Is it somewhere that we dream of going to when finally, our flesh

is cold and dead?

I think I know a secret, or a fantasy, - or maybe an insanity. Perhaps it is a dream?

And yet, my words can never capture Silence, nor Her warm embrace – nor all the things my restless eyes have seen.

Unborn

The guru strives to be unborn.
Just like a child returning to the womb.
Devolving back into a single cell,
Then swimming back into a childless gloom.

He seeks that blessed silence, long before the world was born.
He seeks that peaceful nothingness before the universe was formed.
But, once created, time was never meant to flow back to eternity.
And time is not our enemy, although its gifts are often hard to see.

We were silence once, but now divinity has found a voice.
We were one before, but now we play a multitude of games and live to cast the dice.
Like Yin and Yang, our silence and our voice combine to build each brand-new day.
Where love and loss must pay the cost and everything is play.

Both misery and joy entwine upon this ever-growing vine.
We flow from dark to light and back again along the streams of time.
The stream of time flows not into an ocean, but into the vast expanding reach of space.
And we may never reach a perfect end, because perfection always stays one step ahead, in this – our all too human race.

We strive too hard, and beat our breast in penitence for being simply who we are.

But we are gods reborn – our flesh and bones were made from dying stars.

Perfection is the state we left behind, and who knows when we'll ever find our way.

Perhaps these brief existences we share may lead us home one day?

I do not know, and so I live my life in gratitude for every single day.

I do my best and I accept that being good enough is good enough today.

There is so very much to learn that I must be resigned to live in ignorance and awe.

And yet, within me is a silence which, before the world was born, may well have written Nature's laws.

Methuselah

Methuselah had lived his joyless life for far too long.

It seemed as if he'd laughed at every joke and cried with every song.

The weight of all his years had been a burden much too hard to bear.

If only he had learned to live as an eternal child, -

If only he had learned to live his life without a care.

He was born too soon to know the many different prophets of a nameless god whom man had given many names.

And so, besieged by all the troubles of the world, the old man had forgotten whence he came.

The years had weighed so heavily; such grief - so many wives and children born then lost and gone.

And still the burden of responsibility imprisoned him in his own flesh,

Long after joy or hope, or even any comfort in companionship were gone.

They say he lived a thousand years. They say he was a famous patriarch of old.

A rich old man who spent his life accumulating oxen, wives and land and gold.

But he was never truly young. The gates of Eden were long closed before his birth.

And man had long since learned to slay his brothers and his sisters,

And to grind his neighbours face into the dirt.

Poor Methuselah, - to live a thousand years and never see the face of God.

The choicest wines, the sweetest fruits were his to eat. His many children watched the flocks and turned the sod.

But life is barren and our riches fail to soothe the emptiness inside when we have crushed our inner child.

When we have walled our innocent, eternal nature in a living tomb of mud-build walls, and laws that call compassion crime,

And never see the beauty in a single flower, or feel the heartbeat of the earth, nor learn to live a life that's free and wild.

Wishful Dreams.

I wish I had the words to lance your hidden pain and bring the tears that cleanse the past and bring a brave new day.

I wish I had the words to make you laugh until your tears had dried away.

I wish I knew a way to make you realise that we are never left alone – no matter what the cynics say.

I wish that I could help you see the bright and shining world that lives a moment's kindness or a friendly smile away.

I know perfection lies beyond our reach, beyond our grasp, - but it is still a dream that can be true someday.

I don't have all the answers but I know our hopes and aspirations, and our love will, somehow, find a way.

The many different paths to happiness we see have left us all confused, - our fears and needs have led us all astray,

But I have found that all the kindness I've been shown has made me realise that kindness is our first important step along the way.

I used to wish that I could write a book one day that everyone would read.

A book to help us understand, and finally attain, the many varied things we think we need.

But words are just the limits of our thoughts, and silence holds the answer to our plight.

A sacred silence filled with love, accepting both our darkness and our light.

Kaleidoscope

So many lives, so many dreams.
So many hidden hopes and wishes.
Looking from the outside, -
No one's life is ever as it seems.

The scars so deep, the wounds so raw.
The silent tears that no one ever saw,
The disappointments hidden by a wistful smile,
And yet, somehow, on broken wings, we flew another mile.

Although we care, my pain was never yours, - your pain was never mine.
And mostly, we just kept it to ourselves – pretending everything was fine.
We smile and say hello, and that's a pure-but-simple act of love.
But in the end, the secrets that we even try to share are never fully understood.

Still, maybe, understanding isn't what we really need?
Maybe we can just accept each other's aberrations, follies, or desires and needs?
In acceptance of each other's lives with all their twists and turns.
Maybe we can find a soothing balm for all the pain inside that aches and burns.

Just a Dream…

In every city in the world, the old folk stood with flags unfurled.
Sunlight sparkled on the rails of wheelchairs,
Polished by the effort to sustain a life of chronic inconvenience,
Its fleeting victories now marred by aches and pains.

Many of the menfolk looked a little tired and slightly broken,
Once straight backs were bent and stooped with age,
But the women who supported them looked stronger, - more formidable,
Their scarves and burkas could not hide a lifetime's worth of rage.

If you could only see the banners that they held,
A colourful but ragged, patchwork quilt of broken dreams,
Spread across the streets like petals in the wind,
The flowering of the rage of generations who could never really win.

Nothing moved, and nothing could.
A billion elders blocked the high streets of the world.
While Nike and all her fashionista sisters phoned their favourite politicians,
Even the old men in China thought that sending in the tanks would be absurd.

There are no cover stories when you need a million paramedics to contain a 'riot'.
They tried to re-enlist the veterans as saboteurs, but they were

already gone.
They had squandered most on ill-placed trust and they had been the first in line,
The first to say that change was overdue, and that the world was running out of time.

There were no cardboard signs to tell the politicians what they had to do.
They've known for over sixty years, but sold their souls – as shysters often do.
A billion disillusioned parents told their children, they could do much better -if they tried.
A billion voices swore that they would stop the world until the world had changed, or every one of them had died.

Death of a Narcissist

You tried so hard, - but now he's gone.
So many rights he can no longer wrong.
But even hell can leave an aching void,
A life of hell can leave a bitter emptiness inside.

You try to gather in your scattered dreams.
You try to find the ones he hasn't stained.
Those dreams he stole and turned into a siren song,
To lead you on a rose-strewn path until your precious dreams
were all but gone.

You bore your wounds with hope, as lovers always do,
You told yourself that every rose must have its thorns.
The cutting words and blows were, somehow, always down to
you,
You cried yourself to sleep and woke to tears of penitence with
every hope-filled dawn.

You never were the one to heal him,
Twisted limbs must first be broken to be set anew.
And you were born to be the anvil – not the hammer –
There was very little left that you could do.

Your strength was in your core of steel,
You took so many blows and yet, you never bent.
You freely gave your love to one who never understood the
meaning of the word.
To one who probably will never realise they lost their one slim

chance that Fate had sent,

Who never saw, who'll never see, - that you were Heaven-sent.

Unsung Heroes.

I worked as a picker/packer once.
Racing lines of bottles as they trundled forward to a pit of broken glass.
Raising handfuls to the light to separate the wrong from right.
Filling endless cartons of the chosen to perform a useful task.
How could we drink our whiskey, or our brandy or our gin,
Without a sturdy, well-built flask?

We felt like minor gods, - the power of life or death at our command.
The prestige of the bottling plants was safe within our careful hands.
Then, one day, they found a better way to sort the bottles that we made.
We stood there, idle as they passed us like a glittering parade.
I pushed a button every minute and the new machine would pick a thousand bottles up in one big claw.
I pushed my big red button. It was all that's left to do of what they hired me for.

I quit, of course! And then, I joined the army just to see if I could stand the pace.
Underneath their Jack-boot heels I found a brand-new form of grace.
My body was the beast I learned to master – to obey my masters whims.
I marched and fought. I found a strength I never knew I had.
I found an even greater strength when everything went bad,

And even when I beat my masters at their well-honed game and walked away,
I felt a little sad.

I found a trade and every day I learned a little more.
Pushing hard to earn a little extra every day and reading every night,
Because I knew my life was meant for so much more.
And so, I pondered life until the early hours and grabbed a few hours' sleep,
Before I grabbed my pack-up as I stumbled, weary, out the door.
I had a family to feed, and much too little time to waste on feeling tired and sore.

But I was lucky, I could feel the stars and know that life was so much more.
I could hear the whisper in the trees that told me what my life was for.
I gazed up at the moon and felt her wisdom touch my blood and bones.
I knew I was a star-born minstrel searching for the way back home.
And though I never fit in with this world, or truly felt at ease,
I knew that somewhere past the void, or deep within – there was a place of peace.

And now, I'm thinking of the unsung heroes, - all those men and women that I knew.
They cooked and cleaned and worked themselves into an early grave to pay their daily dues.

I finally came home to share my dreams, but found the friends I'd hoped to save were dead and gone.

Perhaps they never would have listened, or perhaps I simply stayed away too long?

Were there any words of comfort I could give to calm their fears and dry their tears?

I wonder, but I'll never know, because I stayed away for far too many years.

CHAPTER 4 : A PENNY FOR YOUR THOUGHTS.

A penny for your sorrows,
A shilling for your joy.
A nickel for your solitude,
A dollar for your soul.

A thousand pounds for all your worries,
Or a million dollars for your love.
A life of comfort for your wisdom,
But you must never, ever look above.

A nice new car may solve your angst.
A steady income for the blood you spilled.
It doesn't matter if the blood was yours,
The dreams they sell will never be fulfilled.

A Gucci handbag if you never look within,
A new electric Porsche to travel safely through the night.
It drives itself to where you're told to go, -
No need to ever look out to the left or to the right.

I took a penny for my thoughts and bought their dreams for everything I had.
I spilled my blood and ground my bones to earn a crust until I realised that I'd been had.
I wish I'd been a rebel when I'd strength enough to tear apart their lies,

But now I've only strength enough to cry out to the moon,
or gaze out at our brave new world with dumb surprise.

I wish that I could warn the young about the pits and snares that
line their paths.
But they would only see a crazy and unkempt old man or woman
who has way too many cats.
We never have the latest fashions now, we're happy with the
clothes we always wore.
We wore them out, - just like our folly, and it left us with the keys
that open wisdom's door.

For Tina

When we first met, all I had left, was ashes in my hand,
You touched me deeply, in a way, that I may never truly understand.
Heart to heart and mind to mind, as if our very souls were joined,
It seemed that long before we met, our fates already intertwined.

I felt my life was over, in the dark and dismal days before we met,
I was ready then, to leave this, sometimes, bitter world without regret.
You came into my life, and healed my broken heart with patience and with love,
Your friendship came to me, so unexpectedly, a blessing from above.

Although you weren't my first love, in my heart I know that you will be my last,
When I gaze into your deep blue eyes, I know our love will grow, I know our love will last.
Words can never let me tell you just how much you mean to me,
Let me share my life with you, and in time, I know that you will see
the many ways that we both help each other, be the best that we can be,
And how the Love we share may last until Eternity.

The Strangeling

She never chose the path she walked,
Too often, we are never 'going to' and only 'running from'.
And as the evening light was slowly dimming,
All the pretty flowers that kept her company had closed their petals and were gone.

The wind seemed much too soft,
To cause the creaking branches overhead,
The leaves were whispering in the shadows,
But she couldn't understand a single word they said.

The moon peeped through the overhanging branches,
Laying silver light along the dusty road ahead.
A rutted country lane must lead to somewhere,
And the sound of her own footsteps soothed the voices in her head.

She knew she was not bad, but maybe she just wasn't good enough.
The voices told her she was much too soft – sometimes they said she was too tough.
Sometimes they said she was too quiet – sometimes she was too loud.
She only knew that she could never win – she wouldn't be allowed.

But then the voice in the trees called out to her and told her she was free.

They said that if she brought them with her, they would teach
her how to 'be'.
They promised her their wisdom and their love – no matter what
the world might say,
That with their guidance, she'd become the person she was
meant to be some day.

She was not unprepared –
with sturdy boots, a hat and coat,
a backpack with the things she needed,
and the book of poems she wrote.

They helped at first, before the pain became too great to bear,
Before she had to run away,
But now the failing light meant she must find a place to rest,
Until the dawning of the day.

The bridge was much too big for such a tiny river,
And it made a perfect shelter just outside a tiny town.
Perhaps there'd be a place to find some breakfast?
Maybe even somewhere she could settle down?

But she was much too young and kindly hearts would send her
back to hell.
No one listens to the children, Or the stories that they have to
tell.
With promises that she'd behave, that she'd no longer roam,
The kindly policeman took her hand and led her safely home,

The years slipped by and freedom came, but people thought her strange.

She never cared about the things they said or played their silly games.

The voices in her head were kind and taught her things that only angels knew,

And she could heal a wound with spider's webs and cool a fever with the morning dew.

Do They?

I wanted to write a brave dissertation,
On religion and truth, and world depopulation,
On pirates – who once sailed the seven seas,
But who now sell roundup and sterile seeds.
I wanted to put all the facts on display,
But then, - nobody listens too much, anyway!

I was there on that wonderful, hope-filled morning.
That glorious day when the world web was dawning.
An era of truth when all tribes could communicate –
Well, we even got gifted with Google Translate.
I can talk to a friend who's a whole world away.
But then, nobody hears you too well, anyway!

I have friends on the right – I have friends on the left.
(God bless Karl Marx, - and true Christians I've met!)
The Pagans, the Hindus, the Buddhists, - the Fae,
Were all proven right in their own special way.
Last night, I'd a dream that I'd something to say,
But then, no one believes you too much, anyway!

I woke up with a 'secret' that everyone sees,
Our mother, the Earth has been brought to her knees.
Her treasure all stolen, - her coffers laid bare,
To promote a false 'wealth' that is nothing but air.
Imaginary wealth causing deaths that are real,
But the facts are just paper, - unless you can feel.

My point, - If I have one, is easy to see.
Unless we can change, we will soon cease to be.
The world will be fine in the care of the crickets,
Who won't leave their children to die from the rickets.
The ant and the worm will just muddle along,
And the birds that are left will soon sing a new song.

Questions (2023)

Perhaps there are no valid questions?
Maybe, all we have that's real is life?
I've been thinking...
Maybe all my wants and wishes were the cause of all the problems in my life?

I look back at my childhood,
and I realise that I had far too many questions – even then.
My days were filled with thoughts of who and where and why and how and when.
I rarely stopped to listen to the thunder or enjoy the smell of summer after rain.

I lived alone inside my head, and never saw the web of love that weaves the world.
A thousand voices calling me, so many helping hands, whose guiding touch I never felt.
Divination brought its wisdom to my mind, but it never really touched my heart.
To find my life, I had to give my life away and make another start.

Then one day an angel came and help me feel the earth between my feet.
She handed me a drum and helped me feel the rhythm of the earth within its beat.
She handed me a stone and helped me feel the life within its brittle shell,

She took me to the edge of the Abyss, and I released my questions as I fell.

So many questions, but I am content, and I accept that I may never know,
the answers to those childhood mysteries that used to vex me so.
The morning dew, the rising sun, - the distant traffic or the laughter of the children as they play, -
These are the things that make my life worthwhile and bring me gratitude for one more blessed day.

Please Don't Cry

Please don't cry,
Well not unless you really need to wash the pain away.
But, if you cry,
Remember that the pain may never fully go away.

Life is hard sometimes,
Some days we want to scream out to the sky.
Those screams we kept inside too long,
For all times we hurt and never knew the reason why.

It's hard not to remember all those wounds that cut so deep.
We give in to the holding on of all the pain we seem to want to keep.
But if we manage to forget the hurtful things that people say,
We may forget it never was our fault, if we should be accused again someday.

"It takes two to Tango" – people often say.
But sometimes dancers plan the moment of your fall before the music starts to play.
Never be ashamed that you were fooled with words you waited for so long to hear,
The need is written deep into our hearts to find the one who holds us near.

Life is short and hard, but when it flows, our life can be a gift beyond compare.
The secret seems to be in delving deep inside to find the love that

blossoms there.

An inner love that flows out to the world and then returns to warm our hearts a thousand-fold.

A love that guides our life when we are young, and leads us home when we are tired and old.

Transitions

Life is beautiful.
It is not beautiful because of when, or why or where.
It flows out through the universe and scatters all around.
Then it rises from the oceans, up into the clear blue air.
Cycling through the skies, the mountains, the valleys and the ground.
Cycling through the cricket and the worm.
Cycling through the wolf and through the bear.
Cycling through the woman and her tears,
Until the world runs dry.

Life is also terrible.
And this is why our tears must always come.
We who know the stars in the depths of our being,
We who gaze out at the midnight sky in wonder,
We who cry out to the moon in longing,
We who touch the distant stars in wild imagination,
Somehow, know we are immortal beings encased in flesh,
Our minds can reach the vast expanse of possibilities,
With fragile bodies that we see are very soon to die.

What of those who cheat the terror?
Sitting on the side-lines of the endless race of man?
We are racing past them, sweating, swearing, striving,
As they sit there, calmly, with their open, outstretched hands.
Are they just like senseless beasts who feel eternity in every moment of their day?
Or, are they cowards who will not fight and simply run away?

No! They are Gods, like every ant and every worm that wriggles in the ground.

They try to strip away humanity to grasp this peaceful jewel they found.

But soon, their ash will settle and they'll rest, like us, beneath the sacred ground.

I have tried to find an answer to these questions,

And the answer is that, sometimes, - we are free.

Free to live and die in this, our vast potentiality.

Sometimes, free to choose and sometimes free to walk away,

Sometimes free to choose the games that we may want to play.

Natures gives us all the skills that creatures need to just survive.

Parents gift us all the myths we need to keep our mystery alive.

Society provides the chains to keep us firmly in our place.

But we may sometimes choose the way we wish to run this, all too human, race.

Vagabonds.

Let us share our emptiness and let us share our pain.

Let us share the memories we hope, someday, will come again.

Those moments when we touched the world and felt it's warm embrace, -

Those moments when we touched Divinity and felt it's loving grace.

We feel like vagabonds, and thieves, who steal each momentary joy.

We wander hungry and alone beneath a careless sky.

Like orphaned kittens – catching leaves of comfort blowing in the wind,

We gaze into the open doors we pass – that never let us in.

We are wounded warriors who search for that illusive thing called love.

Someone may have told us once, - it falls from somewhere up above.

But all we feel is rain. It soaks our hair and chills our bones.

We wander restlessly. We try to find a place to call our home.

Somewhere, - in this world, or in the many worlds that lie ahead.

We dream of sleeping by a blazing hearth, upon a warm, dry bed.

The warmth of love will dry our bones and take the chill of loneliness away.

And as we drift into a timeless sleep, our lost and lonely hearts will find their way.

Who Am I?

We are stories, we are rhyme.
We are patterns on the page of time.
We are laughter, we are tears,
We are actors on a stage,
We are kindness, we are love,
And sometimes we're children filled with rage.

Sometimes we call this life a journey,
And sometimes we call this life a dance.
For some this life is just a game,
They cast the dice and take the chance.
At times, it seems to me - the gambler's view is very true.
For life may change beyond compare with just a single glance.

But was it worth the visit?
Was it worth the pain?
Is it true that we return again, and yet again?
Is it true that everything in life may be a gain?
The toil, the suffering, the worry and the pain,
The love, the loss – the moments that will never come again?

This is the mystery that drives some men to madness,
The puzzle that so many times has caused the world to burn.
If this piece of life I know as me, goes on for ever?
Why can't I remember who I am when I return?
Am I just a droplet from an ocean of immortal, timeless Being,
Flowing into all of Nature's endlessly evolving dream?

Wishing

I saw you smile as you passed by the other day,
Startled, I returned the smile too late as you looked down.
Too slow, too lost in thought, I missed the chance,
You never saw my wistful, wishful frown.
You carried your embarrassment away without a backward glance.

I battled through the rush of screaming kids, the other day.
Almost catching up, - I walked behind you just to bathe in your perfume,
I didn't dare to touch you – in a daze I wandered on.
Quickly peering back, I saw you walk into your room.
A fleeting glance, and then you closed the door and you were gone.

I wanted to befriend you, on the day you first arrived,
Just to place my tray upon your table in the staff canteen,
A dozen times I walked up to you, just to walk on by,
and not a look, or smile, or word would come,
My need, my love, my shyness, struck me dumb.

I never thought that I could ever feel this way.
Twenty years of marriage, loving husband, happy kids,
When you are near, they all just seem a million miles away,
I must be mad. I realise, that just one kiss, one warm embrace,
and I would throw it all away.

Then today you turned around to see the longing in my eyes.

And as our gazes met, my body trembled with excitement and desire,

The light of longing in your cool green eyes erased my twenty years of lies.

Hand in hand we took a long, slow walk, and found a world I never knew before.

And all the world I thought I knew became a memory of ancient tombs upon a distant shore.

The Secret

The secret burns inside us and our fragile egos fear to touch the flame.
While distant stars remind us who we are and why we came.
We bear the torch of wisdom in a world that soon will fade.
A wisdom that we carry from the cradle to the grave.

In this dance of life, we hold the fire of ancient wisdom high for all to see.
A wisdom poured into the void, creating all that's past and all that's yet to be.
Deep within our hearts we touch a truth that words cannot reveal.
A truth that lives in all we dream and all we try to grasp and feel.

We cannot touch the flame we carry deep within our hearts and blood and bones.
It burns too bright and lights the shadows in our hearts that make us feel alone.
That separation in our souls that carries us through time and space until we reach eternity,
Those bonds of flesh with which we bear our sacred load, is all we know and all we see.

We are the shadow and the light, who journey through this long dark night.
We carry Unity, or Love, – and who can name what has been bound so tight?
This seed of immortality we pass from child to child across the

vast expanse of time.

Living brief, forgetful lives, - creating stories to explain the reason and the rhyme.

On the day that we remember, all we think we know will be consumed by endless light.

On the day that we remember, there will be an end to what we thought was endless night.

On the day that we remember, all we know as pain and suffering will be burned away.

On the day that we remember, God's long dream will end and we will greet a bright new day.

Just An Old Dog

Maybe I've been talking far too much about the things you used to do.
But now I find myself back in the room where we first met, that day.
Your ears were way too big, - they never seemed to fit no matter how you grew.
And now I sit here thinking of the laughter, and the loving years that quickly flew away.

I wasn't very keen on dogs in that old life before you blundered in.
I bought you as the lesser of two evils with a failed deposit on a house.
The other dog that Tina liked was semi-Hell Hound, semi- Djinn.
Kaiser, - A rescue from the pits of Hell, that only Satan would take in.

But there you were, all paws and ears, - with big brown eyes to still my fears.
A safer bet, I felt, all 'round – a gentle soul, a sweet and cuddly family hound.
You were never mine, but we grew old together at the closing of your years.
Slowly plodding round the park, until you'd dive into the bushes for another ball you found.

You loved your cuddly toys – not that they lasted very long.
Apart from that old donkey we were gifted on our evening walk

as we were heading home.

You saw it in a garden and you wedged your mutton head into the fence, - I couldn't move you on.

You wouldn't budge. The owner let you have it and you wagged your way back home.

I miss the way you used to lean that massive head of yours against my thigh.

I'd rub those long hot ears of yours and both of us would sigh together at the beauty of the world.

You saw so much with those brown eyes that I would not have seen alone.

But maybe we can sit and watch the world again, when I have found my way back home.

The Wild Faeries.

Keep your fire and steel, for we are creatures of the mist and air.

Do not seek us in the nooks and crannies of your home, for we were never there.

Distant kin, perhaps – who in the distant past were drawn like wolves into your dreams.

But we are creatures of the earth and stars, and when you called - we never came.

No one from among our clan has ever graced your hearth or home.

Only vagabonds and rogues who walk alone have ever found our home.

There was a prince of ancient myth who loved a Faerie queen.

But one sad day he rode away and never more was seen.

You love your satin sheets and silken shirts too much to walk our way.

You cannot wait to sit before your fire and dream when ends the weary day.

Here among the wild, wide glens there is no comfort for the fearful nor the weak,

But we will shelter the unwanted children and the ones who never speak.

We who sing in words that you can never understand will be the voices for the lost.

We will card our stolen wool to comfort those you count as flotsam and as dross.

We who have no judgement stole away the children you despised.

We who have a different wisdom see your self-indulgent lies.

Keep your metal cities on your stolen lands but leave our final hideaways alone.

We were creatures of delight, but now we haunt the night and you have turned our hearts to stone.

Our mother Earth lies torn and bleeding from the work of greedy, careless hands.

But there is still a chance that you may turn around and heal Her wounded lands.

A Step Away from Tir na N'og

In the distance, I can hear the evening traffic roar.
Still, I dream of days I spent upon that other shore.
The trees still whisper secrets, as they did in 'Tir Na N'og'
Reminding me of ancient lanes, despite the thundering tarmac roads.

I am never far away, no matter where I rest my head.
In my heart, your towering trees will always sway above my exiles bed.
For now, the Willow and the Hazel bring some comfort to my tears.
Your laughter in the wind brings ease, to these – my waning years.

My limbs are not as supple as they were and speed is not my style.
But still, my mind is stronger than the stoutest tree and needs no trickery nor guile.
I walk with patience, and with memories enough to light my grateful smile.
I've learned, my kindness and my truth are all I need to make my life worthwhile.

Thinking back to childhood days, I sometimes wish that they could be returned
But then the fickleness of un-reflected, early adulthood would be yet to be endured.
Besides, the road ahead is all we have to travel and there is no

turning back to start anew.

And who knows what adventures lie ahead before the pennies for the ferryman are due?

Beyond that sacred river lies a world created from the many worlds we knew.

A portal world that leads to many roads, - some ancient and some new.

Of all the journeys and the dances that may lie ahead when I am, once again, renewed,

I hope my final journey from this world will bring me back to you.

Apex

Standing, arms outstretched, upon a mountain top and praying for my wings.
Disappointed, I must walk back down to face a troubled world for yet another day.
Mighty Father, Mother of the world, why did you grant me visions of these things?
You graced me with the eyes of angels, but you cursed me with these feet of clay.

I am grateful for the gift of life your endless love so freely gave.
The Summers spent with supple limbs and eager mind that reached up to the sky.
But Summer's gone and Winters beckons like a cold and open grave.
And still, a lifetime's witness to the suffering of the world has left me asking, "Why?"

Some days, I cannot bear to stay – yet other days I cannot bear to leave.
My broken heart has healed so many times I fear to laugh in case it bursts from joy.
I have sifted through the stories of the world to find a story I believe,
And find myself as destitute of wisdom as I was when I was just a boy.

Maybe silence is the answer – maybe silence is the way to heal the soul?

Maybe silence is the birthplace of our world, and maybe silence is our goal?

Maybe in the quietest moments we can reconnect with hope and love and joy?

Maybe all the wisdom that I need was born with me and simply easier to see when I was just a boy.

The Vigil

She sat near the fire on an old easy chair that terrible, cold winter's night.
The room both impressive and gloomy, in a house that had only known candles for light.
But I sat by the hearth, filled with sadness, as the huge ornate fire gave a flickering glow.
And I waited to say my goodbyes to my Lady – that night she was ready to go.

They say, that the poor hold the mantle of goodness, and my lady had never known want,
But her kindness and wisdom had long won my heart in a way that no vanity can.
And I, who began as a servant, and then became both a student and friend,
Despite all my grief and my horror, was determined to stay to the end.
She coughed, then she smiled as if death was amusing, - a trinket for her to behold.
She told me that she had not always been good – in fact she had often been bold.
"Do you mean as a child?". I asked in surprise, as I never once witnessed her faults.
But she croaked out a laugh that sent chills down my spine, then she quietly mentioned her vaults.

"Do you think that the fortune that lies in my vaults came from kindness and care for the poor?

There is blood on the hands of my forebears, and that blood's still a stain on my door.

But long before that I have memories, that some have mistaken for dreams,

Of lives where I died full of anger and pride and my swords had left dark, bloody streams."

"But I'm hoping this life is my last one, and that soon I will go to my rest.

To live a good life is not easy, but I feel I have finally mastered the test."

Her eyes fluttered closed and she left me, to a world I knew little about.

But often I feel her around me, when I'm burdened by worry and doubt.

It's only Valentine's Day

I wasn't going to bother, after all it's just a money-making game.
People taking time off being ass-hats, - just to go and do it all again.
But then, I thought of all the lovely things you do,
And all the lovely ways and means you have of being you.

I hate to say it on this feckless day, but I must admit you are the centre of my life.
On any other day, I find it easier to say how glad I am to have you in my life.
You make each day seem brighter and you make my burdens light.
One day would never be enough to thank you for the fun, the laughter and delight.

I really hate to bother, when it's only one short day,
One day of all the years we had - those years I hope will never pass away.
But you will always be my world until my world grows cold.
For on this day of gilt and glitter, I still have a love that's gold.

CHAPTER5: SLIPPING AWAY

Sometimes, I like to slip away to where the Elves and Fairies play.
Where Dragons cast their wind-swept shadows on the ground,
Flickering past where tall green grasses dance and weave and sway,
And nothing but the present moment matters anyway.

Sometimes, the forest or the mountains seem too far away.
The warm and sunny beaches are a journey for another day.
My body doesn't want to leave its present place of rest or ease,
And so, I take a long, deep breath and simply slip away.

It is no crime to simply dream a life that's yet to be.
To dream a life that never was, is just my cup of tea.
The dreamers build a better world that may come true, someday,
So, it's no crime to let our burdens fall for just a while, and simply slip away.

The land of Fae is just as real as any thoughts with which we fill our minds.
But in that land of song and joy our long-lost youth awaits.
Why stress and worry? We can slip away from all that chafes, or aches, or binds.
Just take a journey to the Land of Youth and Joy, to see what we may find.

Ordinary Lives

There are no ordinary lives.
There is Life, the Universe, the Dance.
There is no destiny that Fate has carved in stone.
There is Need and there is Hope and there is Chance.

Sometimes we sense the warp and weave,
Sometimes we sense the road ahead.
Some people spend a lifetime gazing at the stars,
Some people tend each other's needs, instead.

We are not Wise, but we are part of Wisdom.
We are not Good, but Goodness fuels our very being.
We do not clearly see the path ahead,
But every path we walk is clearly seen.

How can every act be random, - but the way ahead be sure?
There is a need within the casting of the dice, - the need for Love
and more.
Freedom is the mother and the child of Love – the future's open
door.
When the Dance is over, we will understand what all our pain
was for.

There are no ordinary lives, - just Freedom on Her way to finding
Love.
There are no wasted lives, - there are no final condemnations
from above.

In this Chrysalis we call the Universe, the future grows from everything we do.

The Butterfly, - that many call the 'Risen Universe', is part of them, and me, and you.

We Win ...We Lose.

Roll the dice or deal the cards. The game's the only thing.
Chase that rainbow over hills or sodden sun-swept glens.
Draw an ace, or win first place – or grasp that golden ring.
The only certain truth of life is when the winning ends.

Maybe there's another game among those greener pastures of our dreams.
Maybe there's a Heaven or Valhalla where and angel or a maiden sing?
Surely when we clear the table with our winning hand, our dream is all it seems?
But no matter how much gold we grasp – that bell of doom will ring.

I can hear its hollow chime. It peals out in the marshes of my mind.
Sunny pools and sodden bracken underneath a rainbow – painted, clear blue sky.
I gaze in wonder at the passing clouds and splash my way across a day so fine,
But on the final tolling of the bell, I realise its call is just for me.
And I already know the reason why.

An alter made of warm black stone gives comfort to my aching bones.
My pounding heart is stilled by gentle wind and warming sun.
I take this time of stillness to remember all the deeds for which I

must atone.

And yet, I feel completed and content although the bells have said my time has come.

I am wondering at the times I tried too hard to win, although it doesn't really matter anymore.

But I can hear the splashing of its oars as that last ferry, with its ghostly gondolier, draws near.

Nothing here seems so important when your soul is gazing at that other shore.

My one regret? - I never laughed enough. But now I am content, and feeling neither misery nor fear.

I look back at my worn-out body with a condescending smile.

I really looked a mess, I guess that I was never blessed with style.

But ego is a set of habits I have left behind that Nature etched into our muscles and our brains.

And though my life was rather fun, I need a little rest – before I cast the dice again.

A Toast to New Year's Day

Some of us have slept the new year in,
And some have partied all night long.
So, as we face another New Year's Day,
Let's raise a glass to help the year along.

Here's to those who dream of endless roads that never reach an
end.
Here's to those who walk alone – who dream of long-lost friends.
Here's to those who walk the path where lonely visions lead,
And here's to those who find their way back home, and those
who follow love – no matter where it leads.

Here's to those who dream of mansions, or a quiet cottage by a
little stream.
Here's to those who dream of sunlit beaches where the weary go
to rest and dream.
Here's to those who lay upon the forest floor and kiss the sacred
earth.
And here's to those who dream of castles in the sky, and even if
they never learn to fly – they live a life of mirth.

Here's to those of us who wonder what may lie ahead, - for no
one ever truly knows.
We dream of comfort and security, but time and tide will never
cease to flow.
Good and bad may come in turn and we may never know which
one is which for sure,
So let us raise our glasses to another year – the future is an ever-

open door.

I Once Met An Elf With A Slow, Winning Smile.

I once met an elf with a slow, winning smile.
He walked with a limp, but he dressed in great style.
He was taller than most – well about two-foot-three,
And he wore a long sword than went down to his knees.

I had just passed the mines where the seven dwarfs toiled,
Before they got lazy and round and well-oiled.
Considerably wealthy since 'Cindz' made it big.
They all drank like fish and they all ate like pigs.

I shook my head sadly to see their old hut,
Entangled in cobwebs and covered with dust.
The elf called me over between his long sighs,
He told me his fear of the Dwarves loves of pies.

This elf was a count, and a doctor to boot.
He was well versed in music and played a fine flute.
His life had been wondrous! His life had been fine,
Until his wife, Tiffany, got trapped down a mine.

He'd heard that the Dwarves had abandoned their trade,
But he hoped they would honour past deals they had made.
He needed some diggers to dig his wife out.
But his old friends, the Dwarves had become much to stout,

We went to the castle and found those old miners,

To find they were covered in bruises and shiners.
A row had begun when old Grumpy had said,
They were all gone too lazy, and fat, and well-fed!

Well, even old Happy had gotten the hump.
And a row had begun when old Grumps got a thump!
Although battered and bruised, they were happy to help,
And they grabbed the old picks gathering dust on a shelf.

It was a long walk to the old count's estate.
The Dwarves sipped on water and nibbled on dates.
They grew lean and fit as our party trekked on.
When we got to the mine, all their tummies had gone.

They slipped down the mine and they quickly set to.
We knew they'd succeeded, when they shouted "WOO HOO!
The countess was grimy, and had broken her nails,
But she'd kept herself fed on some mushrooms and snails.

We had a big party for Christmas that year,
With truffles and souffles and brandy and beer.
But the Dwarves nibbled carrots and lettuce and cheese.
They had learned to adapt to their new life of ease.

Bucket List

There were so many things that I wanted to do,
There are some that I've managed quite well.
But I wanted a poem without 'old-fashioned' rhyme,
I guess that didn't go very well!

I woke up today looking back on my life,
The bits that are finished - at least…
Now I gaze out the door of this once-posh hotel,
And I've learned to be grateful for peace.

My thoughts upon waking, - and maybe asleep,
Were about all the vows that we make and we keep,
About all the dreams in our life that came true,
And the blessings we never once thought would accrue.

I know I've been lucky – my age tells me so,
As I gaze at this carpark that's sprinkled with snow.
A new page unopened – the future untold,
Here's hoping the god's truly favour the bold!

I spent most my life trying to build a safe nest,
But the times that were scary were likely the best.
The times that I fought and the times I have won,
The times I have lost and have had to move on.

So many positions, locations and roles,
So many 'Me's', you could say? - I suppose…

And so many losses and tears and regrets,
Yet so many friends I will never forget.

I felt them around me as soon as I typed,
Those friends who had sheltered and lightened my life.
Too many to mention – too few to forget.
And they seem to be saying, I'm not finished yet!

Perhaps one last chapter to add to my life.
Perhaps just a small one, with not too much strife?
If troubles appear, I will show them the door.
I will know them on sight! I have met them before...

I still have my wits and what's left of my health.
And I'm happy enough with the cards I've been dealt.
So, a new page is opened, the old pages read...
And there's nothing to do but to press on ahead!

THE KING OF THE BEGGARS

The hounds had lost the scent and circled fearfully around a pile of rags beneath a holly tree.
Their lust for blood was gone – the hunt had gone all wrong, but neither lords nor ladies understood what it might be.
The master cursed beneath his breath – his face was red, and dripping sweat – this day might cost him dear.
He kicked the pile of stinking rags with anger, - an anger which was fed by greed and fear.

The rags unfurled into a giant of a man with half-crazed, staring eyes.
His roar of outrage made the horses bolt and hounds retreat in panic and surprise.
The beggar took a long deep breath and gazed around with eyes of piercing blue.
The master of the hunt regained his poise and shouted, "This is private land! Be off with you!"

The beggar bent down slowly, and he picked his wooden bowl up from the ground.
"This land was mine before the likes of you befouled its sacred ground.
You stole the common land from me four hundred years ago,
And left my children with no place to grow their food, - no place to rest, - no place to go!"

"I see it in your hearts. You wish to strike me down and bury me beneath this hallowed ground.

Well. strike with all your might and see how beggar-men can fight when they are run aground!

You grind the poor beneath your heels and steal their homes and hope and bread.

It seems to me that you'll not be content until my children are all dead!"

A flash of movement and an oaken staff appeared, as if by magic, in the beggar's rugged hands.

"Come to me now and I will fight you for my home, my children and my lands!"

The skies grew dark and all the sons and daughters of the rich began to shake with fear.

Their sweating palms and groaning bowels presaged, - the time of retribution had drawn near.

They quickly rode away and tried to make-believe that it had been just play.

A crazy beggar who had spoiled the hunt and chased the hounds away.

But in the silence of the night, they woke from dreams about an army of the poor.

An army who reclaimed the land which had been stolen by their kindred many years before.

Magical Millicent

We rarely get to meet the Headless Horseman or the Banshee
these fine days.
The Gentle folk don't walk the lonely country lanes – except on
special days.
The traffic screams by day and night – no Leprechaun is safe.
And the Gentle Folk were never known to just sit back and chafe!

They have taken to the world wide web and now they chat on
Zoom.
And they weave a web of magic with no need for wool nor looms.
While ancient Fairies stand and glare or push the tourists down
the stairs.
The young ones rule the ethernet, and play their pranks on
there!

The modern fairies seldom have a castle or a circle of their own,
The slightest grasp of graphics is enough to build themselves a
vast palatial home.
They slip into our online games and steal our time away.
How often have you gone online to check your mail, and been on
there all day?

They love to play with passwords because portals are their
thing.
They rule the login pages and they may not let you in.
And then, when you reset the password, they will change it back
again...
"I am sorry but you used that word before – it can't be used

again!"

Again, when online shopping when you find that 'must-have' dress,
The shopping cart won't open and you pound the keys with stress.
When finally, you get it to open – it's no longer in your size,
When someone tells you, "It's the Fairies" - do not be surprised.

When I met Millicent, I thought that she was just another troll.
Her wit so sharp, her logic so unworldly and her humour was so droll.
She told me all about the younger fairies who had learned to live online.
She said the world was now their oyster and their future looked just fine.

They tune into the 5G signal and they zip from tower to tower.
She said this modern century would be their finest hour.
I said I had my doubts about the stories that she told,
But then she tapped my head, the screen went dead, - the room went dark and cold.

On Passing a Leprechaun.

I want to write a silly poem, but I wonder of it's in me?
I write about the faeries and I don't want them 'agin' me…
The Faeries are such Gentle Folk – So kind and full of mirth,
But if I don't get the tone quite right – I'll end up eating dirt!

It's not that they're vindictive! That really isn't true.
But if you pee the wee folk off – there'll, be a day you'll rue!
They never break a promise and they always pay their debts,
And I'm afraid I might get in too far beyond my depth.

I remember Peter Murphy, who thought it was a laugh,
To grab a passing pixie and to throw him in the bath.
The Pixie turned into a dog and bit him on the ass,
And now old Pete has learned to let all passing Pixies pass.

That doesn't sound too bad you say? Well, there was Mary Flynn.
A Faerie knocked upon her door, on wash-day, and she would not
let him in.
He flew up to her chimney and he blew right down the stack.
And from that day poor Mary's smalls were always sooty black!

Then there was Parson Percival – a saintly man, they say.
He found some Brownies in the churchyard and he chased them
all away.
They turned his whiskey into milk and then his milk turned
sour.
And from that day poor Percy was a man both grim and dour.

So, if you see a Leprechaun when out to take a walk,

Be always sure to tip your hat and never stand and gawk.

A smile might help, and maybe a "Good Morrow!" as you quickly stride away.

And never, ever try to join the Good Folk as they play!

Twinsel - A Yuletide Visit.

The first time I saw Twinsel, she looked just like any other elf.
A granny version of the guy they stick up on a shelf.
She didn't have that smarmy grin that made me want to flush him.
With braided shawl – she looked just like a slimmer version of a charming Russian doll.

"You mustn't mention Russia! They'll think I favour Putin! –
You know I can't be doing with that shouting and that shooting!"
I saw the twinkle in her eye and knew that she was teasing,
And for a thousand-year-old lady – to the eye she was quite pleasing.

I didn't wonder why she came – I thought I was still dreaming.
I gazed in admiration at her hair – on which the moon was gleaming.
Her walking stick was thin and black, and tipped with gold and silver,
I gasped to see that she had no reflection in the mirror.

"Do you have a message, mother dear, that I can put in rhyme?"
She stood, and tapped her cane and stared at me for just the longest time.
Was she thinking, - could she trust me with the words that she had come to say?
Or was it best to wait to find a better vessel, or come back another day?

Breathlessly, and full of hope, I waited as her eyes bore into mine.
What were the secrets Twinsel would impart to me to share with all mankind?
Would she echo all the memes we see that ask us all to never be unkind?
Or would she pour the wisdom of the ages into my awaiting mind?

She stole some grapes and manifested cheese to make a snack.
Then she turned and left and never once did she look back.
I know her name was Twinsel, as she spelled it out with pips.
But not one word of wisdom had been gifted by her lips.

Twinsel's Return

Twinsel came again last night – her silver hair a cloud of light.
It was another of those crisp, cool evenings lit by sister moon.
A poor man's altar, laid with purple grapes on clean white lace
and flickering candle light.
A year had passed since she had swept my soul away, one fateful,
frosty night.

A poet's hope and dreams laid bare, beside a window - opened to
the cool night air,
Stolen was a heart that once had beat without a worry nor a care.
All rhyme and reason gone astray, no rest since she had gone
away,
And somehow, someone who'd forgotten how to pray was knelt
in fervent prayer.

What can a poet be without their words, their vision and their
own sweet muse?
Days are empty – nights are bare and all is misery and dark
despair.
Words had left me silent. All I had were memories of eyes of
violet-blue.
Without her gifts, I'd nothing left in life to choose – I'd nothing
left to gain and nothing left to lose.

Sleep had long become my enemy, since all my dreams had
strayed.
With window opened every night I knelt in hopeless hope and
dreamed of endless light.

And there she stood – the vision who for such a long, long time I'd prayed.
I thought my wounded heart would burst from inexplicable delight.

Like a rabbit, frozen by the light, I watched her form from starlit night.
Still upon my knees like some uneducated pilgrim from the past.
My mind was fluttering like a leaf - my heart was pounding both in love and fright,
The almost-tears that glistened in my eyes were not enough to wash away the empty year I'd passed.

A simple kiss upon my forehead was enough to heal my year of pain.
She touched my cheek and gazed into my eyes, and then she slipped away.
My long-lost words flowed down like honey as my voice returned again.
My soul regained, and yet, inside a hope still burned that she'd come back some day.

The First Story Teller

Long before the mountains,
Long before the seas.
Long before the evening stars
that bring our souls such ease.

At the dawning of the ages,
Long before the world was new,
The ancient story teller
spoke the only word he knew.

That single word she heard
which broke the silence of the void,
Made the universe reverberate with love
and yearn to be his bride.

But innocence is certain to be lost
When love is fashioned into flesh.
And in the weave of love and flesh and lies,
There lay the path to misery and death.

But the story teller had as many children,
As the dust of every single shining star.
And their stories filled with bravery and fears
Would bring him comfort in his waning years.

Each story shaped a life before that life was born -
It shaped each single day before the coming of the dawn.
But the stories that their parents told his children,

could be changed – A child could be reborn.

The ancient stories, forged when once the world was young,
Could be retold in truth and love – a new and better world begun,
Our childhood lies could be revealed, and then reviled and cast away,
And we could forge the stories of our lives anew, and live in our own way.

CHAPTER 6 : AT THE EDGE OF TRUTH

Standing at the edge of truth, I reach the end of all desire.

Torn between the frozen wastes and all-consuming fires.

Sometimes, dancing in the woodlands, with the spirits of the lands.

Sometimes, praying to a deity who, maybe, understands.

Dabbling at the fringe of science where memes and madmen meet.

Smiling at the people as I pass them on the street.

Reading helps to hone my mind and leave my past mistakes behind,

But when I wander to the edge of what I think I know – I wonder what I'll find?

As I leave my little life behind, my 'knowledge' falls apart when face to face with the eternal truth.

My memories are swept away, - the arrogance of age – the follies of my youth.

As I watch them scatter in the wind like leaves, my voice is also carried far away.

But now my foolish thoughts are gone – I just don't feel like talking, anyway...

Gazing out into the silent darkness, all my pain and all my victories have lost their sting.

They are somewhere in the silence, wandering like sheep

without a shepherd who can gather them back in.

As I breathe out all I knew as 'Me' into the endless void, eternity is calling me away.

But my restless body longs to walk the Earth a little longer, and I sigh a little as my vision fades away.

Seamless

What if life was seamless? Dreamless?

What if it provided everything that we desired?

What if every day was just another carnival parade?

Every moment ticking off the list of all the pleasured that we craved?

Everybody living in a palace filled with all the wealth they have displayed?

Everyone content from all the helpful answers to the prayers that they all prayed?

Every goal, and everything we ever wanted - all ambitions reached and all our hankerings fulfilled?

Wouldn't everyone we know be grateful and so happy, and so chilled?

I doubt it...

Lay Me Down

Let me lay down in the company of those who reached into the void and almost touched the hand of God.
I have seen the Virgin's tears and heard the nails that shook the pillars of the ancient world.
Standing underneath a darkened sky as howling winds cried out against the crimes of Rome.
Her absolution never quite complete – before her sins were fully washed away - her demons came back home.

And yet, she was my mother. She who took me by the hand when I was much too young to understand,
She taught me everything she thought a boy must know, if he would, one day, be a man.
I cannot curse the womb that bore me – nor the eyes that showed me how to see the world.
Without Her sight – I would be blind, and with the wisdom of her words I learned my truths and all I deemed absurd.

Reflected truth is not a lie. The sunlight strikes a prism and is seen upon a different day and by another eye.
The colours may seem different, and all the beauty that we saw depended on the beauty in the viewer's eye.
We gazed in wonder at the star-filled skies and gave our children stories that were never told as lies.
We took the magic in our hearts and wove a canopy of dreams to answer all their 'how's' and all their 'why's'.

I learned the stories of the world, but what is deep within our hearts is that which lies beneath us in the land.

My sacred truths are mine – as yours are yours, - and this is something we must understand.

My sacred spirits live beneath the land where I was born, and here is where I need to be to touch that Spirit's hand.

Your Sacred Spirit's light shines bright, and lies above the skies of sunlit, foreign lands.

Neither truth are lies and there will never be a time when you and I must both agree.

What you see and feel, belongs to you, and what I think I know, belongs to me.

We can be a family of many creeds and all the colours of the rainbow, - if we choose to be,

In a world where everyone is loved and everyone is free.

Between the Warp and Weave

I can almost feel it, - like a tiny gap between each moment of the day.
Between the warp and weave of life, I sense a microscopic rift where I can slip away.
In the pause between each breath there is a momentary freedom I may seize,
A chance to grasp eternity – a chance to grasp a moments rest and ease.

There is blessed silence in that sacred space, a pathway to a consecrated place,
Where all our dreams may follow in the footsteps of divine, eternal grace.
In that formless world where gods and goddesses reflect our own true face,
And all we have become is good enough to take our rightful place.

This fleeting world we face each day has many rules by which the ruled must play.
These fragile bodies long for longer life and co-create the rules we must obey.
But in the silence of eternity where every song we sing is beautiful and true.
The gods and goddesses create a world that's made from everything we do.

Everything that we imagine can exist beyond the limitations of this little life.

But in this life is where our dreams are made amid the challenges and strife.

Every heartbeat is a gift, and every conscious thought a flowering of Divinity within.

We are the flower through which divinity creates the world without, and all the worlds within.

The Beggar

It was the coat that drew me to his side, that cold September day.
He leaned against the wall, inside a porch that barely kept the wind and rain away.
An army coat, just like my dad's, that came back from the war.
I hoped it kept him just a warm as it kept me so many years before.

I dropped some coins into his cup to ease my passage, as I walked away.
But as I glanced into his eyes, I watched him struggle with some words he had to say.
"God is bleeding into life", he said. "And life is struggling to escape the mud.
There is nothing in this world which can be made without our sweat and tears and blood!"

His aura stank of urine and insanity, and so, I walked away until he called me back.
"Your poetry is shite!", he said, "You write of flowers and butterflies like some insipid hack!"
"What can you know, old man, of what I do and who I am?"
He said, "I've walked the lonely roads since mankind first began"

"You think that speaking nice and being good will save you from your misery and pain,
But you will walk as many roads as I and birth will come again and yet again.

Your life may be a fairy tale, but fairy tales are born in blood and
sweat and slime.
The grimy, gritty glories of this world will last until the very end
of time."

"**Y**ou bore me with your godly prayers and clean-pressed
trousers on the shiny pews.
You tire me with your candles and your bells and all your failed
attempts to be a better 'you'
You drive me to distraction with your chanting and your
whistles and your drums.
The only truth is you, - and what you do is what your life
becomes."

"**I** became this world which we both walk and we both share.
Each moment of my birth was made of misery and pain and dark
despair.
You bleed my blood and cry my tears for you and I are one.
This is the mystery which Man has wondered at since Mankind
was begun."

"**F**orget your worries and your foolish plans and simply be!
You never will be greater than you are, for I am you and you are
me.
The measures and the rules with which you gauge your lives are
false beyond compare."
I closed my eyes to still my spinning head, but when I looked
again, he was no longer there!

What Can We Do?

What can we do with all the memories of friends and family that we have left behind?
Those thoughts we wish we could avoid because of all the pain that we may find...
The loves we thought would last forever and the friends we thought would never go away,
They lie upon my heart like lead – these thoughts that steal the lightness from my day.

I wish that I was careless, thoughtless – like a child before the age of three.
Free of baggage, unconcerned with thoughts of who I really ought to be.
Meditation helps for just a while, - it gives some moments to my day when I am free,
But soon enough the memories of all that I have lost come flooding back to me.

Are we crazy to believe that we must bow to all that life can send our way?
Must we bend to every storm, while mumbling that 'each dog will have their day'?
Is acceptance just the coward's way, or is it right to fight and clear our name?
Knowing that the stories people tell themselves will never really change.

In the end, the only judgement that should matter is the one we place upon ourselves.

But sometimes rules are written in our hearts that place an unfair burden on our souls.

Like Anubis, we must weigh our hearts against a feather and release the loads that weigh us down.

Being good enough is good enough, if we would live our lives without a constant frown.

On Being a Lesser Voice

Perhaps we are a lesser voice?
Speaking out from lesser lives, and
Wondering what our world will bring today.
We stall the morning from our beds,
Shuffling problems in our heads,
The cards we choose decide the games we play.

Greatness calls us,
But the lives of heroes can be grim.
Nothing left for us when all the chips are gathered in.
Far too many heroes hung from trees,
With painful deaths, or lives bereft of ease,
For people who will never live in peace.

We want to help,
We want to change the world.
The cards laid out before us seem to show the way.
And as we settle back to sleep,
With mental lists of plans and promises to keep.
The brave new world we dreamed just slips away.

Listening to the Wind

I never really listened to the wind before - the way I did today.
I never stopped quite still enough to hear the secrets that she had to tell.
Her kisses falling on my face just took my breath away.
And then, finally, into her long-awaited cool embrace, I fell.

Was it love or just a dream? How can a mortal really know.
I fell into her arms and I was taken far away.
It seemed as if she took me where my heart was meant to go,
But I am frozen still from her embrace and cannot truly say.

In her grasp I flew, and caught the scent of summers blooms.
Spinning like a feather in her power, the world I knew was swept away.
I tried to cage her feral heart and leash her to my foolish dreams
But who can tame the rushing wind, or hold her in their sway?

I listened to the wind today and all I thought I knew was simply swept away.
She carried me on disembodied wings, through hills and canyons in the skies.
She whispered secrets known to few, until she left me at the end of day.
I sat and cried, and then I tried, but could not write a single word of all she had to say.

I Really Wanted to Believe in Christmas

I really wanted to believe in Christmas, when the sight of witches burning made me want to cry.
How could I accept a faith that meant so many unbelievers had to die?
Santa Claus was kind of cool and every kid is happy to receive some brand-new toys,
But even at the age of seven , all I saw were clouds, when I looked hopefully up to the skies.

I really wanted to believe a world of love existed somewhere – other than in dreams.
Well, mostly, it was me I was concerned about, of course. Our philanthropic thoughts are never what they seem.
I believed, - If I loved you and you loved me – our lives would work out fine.
Then our problems and our differences could all be ironed out with patience and with time.

Somehow, someone as naïve as I have been survived for more than sixty years, and hardly ever tried to end it all.
Sixty-five in fact if we can count the first few blissful years before the blinds of childhoods dreams must fall.
When finally, I realised how much of what we once believed was just another optimistic dream,
Kindness was the only answer I could find, - when looking back at my own life to figure out exactly what it means.

If I'm Gone Away

Promise me you'll stay the same sweet child within that you have always been.
The world can sometimes steal the sweetness from our hearts and take away our dreams.
Choose the paths you'll walk with care – the company you keep will always set the scene.
Looking back, I realise that every place I stayed became a part of everything I've been.

Know your power, and see that every single thought and every single word you say comes true.
You will build you world from every promise that you break and everything you do.
Like a mirror, sometimes we reflect the laws and morals we encounter every day,
But knowing our humanity from deep inside will lead us down a kinder, surer way.

Do not cast your joy up to the heavens to await a day that may not ever come to pass.
Pleasure may be placed aside for just a little while, but happiness is something that will last.
Finding friends that share your dreams will turn a pilgrimage into a carnival parade.
Of all the treasures in my life, my friendships where the greatest gifts it gave.

Many people speak of love but few will understand exactly what it means.

And I would not deprive you of those moments when our lives become a dream.

But in the warm, wild rush of our romantic flings, this truth must still apply, -

The ones to whom we give our hearts will hold a portion of our lives until our dying day.

Hold a space inside for love, but know the greatest love you hold must be for you.

Then, the love you give to others will be real – you'll find the love you have to give is true.

Listen to my words and know – no matter what they tell you – we will meet again someday,

The universe is stranger and more beautiful than anything our prophets or our scientists have to say.

I'm Sure It Wasn't Me

I spoke to someone in my dreams. I'm sure it wasn't me.

Although we seemed to share a fondness for strong rum and builder's tea.

We had much more in common as the hours of conversation flew,

My newfound friend just seemed to have such insights into everything I knew.

We talked about our lives with all their varied ups and downs.

About the things that made us laugh and everything that made us frown.

We weighed our troubles in the balance – allocating blame,

And when we shared our calculations, our results were much the same.

We both agreed the circumstances of our birth were the beginning of our woes.

With better parents who could guess how far such geniuses could go?

A better diet might have added height and strength and width.

And who can say to what outrageous lengths we could have gone with this?

With perfect teeth, we may have smiled our way to fame and wealth and joy.

A little bit of fiscal help from daddy gives a certain boost to every girl and boy.

Some contacts, or some rich and kindly uncles might have

helped to pave the way,

Into a life where every moment brought new opportunities for profit and for play.

But then, the one we never like to mention came along and spoiled our little game.

Like some begrudging spirit of times past, she showed us how our lives would be the very same.

She showed us born of wealthy parents and a life of sloth and ease that led us far astray.

And how we managed to succumb to all the vices we already have – just in a different way.

We still can't say we like her, but we can't deny her point was hammered home.

Like every self-made man and women, every trouble in our life was all our very own.

Crafted from our dreams and fears and made from everything we did or didn't do,

And since that awful dream, we had to take the blame and start our lives anew.

It's just a silly poem and I'm certain there is nothing here that's true.

'Cos if it was, there are so many things I'd really have to change – so much I'd have to do.

I didn't get to where I am today by taking blame for everything, I've done...

And yet, I'm gazing at the mirror and I'm wondering if I really am the one?

CHAPTER 7: THE GREEN MILE REVISITED.

"I'm tired boss". No one with a heart could hear this line and fail to feel it ache with love.

Are we not also poised between both death and life. A cold dark hell below, while heaven waits above?

We walk that long green mile, and for the fortunate among us it is often hedged with joy.

But soon enough, the journey sees its end and then, we stand beside eternity and ask the reason why.

For me, that question never strayed. For all my life it echoed in my mind.

I read the banned and banished books to see what secrets I could find.

I wandered down so many rabbit holes that I completely lost my way.

But when you lose your mind while searching for the truth – it always finds it way back home someday.

When you were raised on made-up mysteries, and slept upon a pillow filled with lies.

The clouds of madness pass before your eyes while searching for the skies.

But when the clouds of madness pass, your mind is calm and clear.

And lies become a stench that can cannot be concealed, or justified by anger or by fear.

Truth is all that you have left when you leave everything you think you know behind.

Every word becomes a web, and ties you to an ancient world that wraps its chains around your mind.

In your new-found ignorance, the world may learn to shine again before your child-like eyes.

In the still and silent place behind your mind, a child may yet be born whose futures lies beneath more kind and sunny skies.

What is there to lose when all the games we played no longer bring a song of gladness to our hearts?

What is there to lose if we have all but reached the end and we are ready for a brand-new start?

What is there to lose, if all the lies we've heard a thousand times before no longer turn our heads?

Are we not fit to be the heralds of a bright new world, when all our hopes for this old world are dead?

Elijah and the Clown.

I dreamt I was a prophet once, with eyes that blazed with wisdom and a tongue so sharp, it cut the strongest bonds with truth.

I dreamt I was Elijah, sent to free the old and foolish from the lies with which they had been so enslaved since they had neither sense nor tooth.

I thought my clear and childlike eyes were given to me as a gift from far beyond the dark and moody, sullen skies that dimmed the land.

But the spiderwebs of wisdom which I tried to catch with clumsy hands were merely dreams and never had the fire that comes with every Deity's commands.

My wistful, wishful visions were just dreams of better worlds that could not stand the garish light of day.

For every one who touched my dreams a thousand turned their heads and simply walked away.

Someone told me, long ago, the one-eyed man would rule the kingdom of the blind.

I tried to sell my dreams, but in the marketplace of life there was no buyer I could find.

Now I paint some laughter on my face and wear the bright apparel of a clown.

The world may bring me to my knees but it will never knock me down.

My will gets stronger every day as youth and vigour fade away.

And as the game gets tougher it incites my will to play.

Cast your dice each morning – there is nothing else to do.

Spread your seeds of kindness and of light for those who follow you.

Death may have the final laugh, or Death may be a door we're passing through.

But it really doesn't matter if He finds you laughing at the funny ways you found out to be you.

The Secret

I want to share an open secret but I cannot find the words to match the way I feel.

It's a secret everybody knows, but many have forgotten, through the worries and the problems of the day.

It's a secret that we know, - about what makes our lives worthwhile, and everything that's real.

It's a secret deep inside our hearts and souls, which may be clouded, but will never go away.

Some days we wake up with that secret shining in our hearts to greet the day.

Those times when life flows smoothly and our health is good and all the world seems bright and gay.

Some days the secret fills us with a joy that makes is feel that joy will never go away.

And yet, the secret is more hidden in those times when everything in life just seems to go our way.

It has always seemed the strangest irony in life to find the secret hidden deeper when our lives are filled with joy.

Forgetfulness is easy when the ship of life sails smoothly on a calm and placid sea.

We all know times when life seems easy and we quickly hide away those things which made us cry.

And in those times a life of comfort is the only life we want, - the only life we see.

But even in the best of times, remember all the tears and all the pain that made you who you are.

The knives from which your strength and individuality were carved, were bound to leave a scar.

The spark of the divine is beautiful, and irresistible when shining in the faces of the unformed young,

But as the spirit grows, the scars of life shine brighter and more vibrant than the noonday sun.

Be proud of every blow and every loss, and every tear that made you who you are.

Each trickle down your cheeks has carved a being of light from dust, long carried from the distant stars.

You are the universe, and you are tied by essence to each lake and stone and tree.

This life is both the hammer and the anvil which has forged the person you were meant to be.

The World Is Doing Fine

The world is doing fine and you can rest your wearied grip upon the wheel.
Fair winds blow the ship of life upon an even course – no matter how we feel.
The storms are real, but none will tear her sails nor crush her hull upon the jagged rocks.
Let go the tiller of a ship that you can never steer – it's time for resting and for taking stock.

It is time to count your tears and let them wash the age-old pains away.
Sadly, there will soon enough be cause for fresh new tears as Nature wends her careless way.
Tears will come and tears will go – just as the year must have its share of rain and wind and snow.
But Spring will always come again, and with it, all the joys that only Springtime knows.

The little life you know as 'me' will come and go like autumn leaves that die upon the trees.
The greater life that guides your every move is rooted deeply in the vast expanding space we call eternity.
Our thoughts and feeling ebb and flow, and drift along with life's relentless tides.
But at our heart, there lies the ancient tree of life, where our immortal soul resides.

When the storms of life wash all you ever knew into the

towering, roaring, waves that hide the very sun.

When you fear to lose that tiny life that you once thought would be your only one,

In the darkness of the raging tempest that now seems to be your only life,

Breathing deeply, touch that ancient tree inside your heart and feel the rhythm of your inner self that lies beyond all pain and strife.

In that sacred, silent moment you will find the eye of every storm in life that howls with vain and futile rage.

In that silence you will find a new direction on the path of life, and light the dawn of a new age.

Whatever new directions that may lie ahead are yours, and yours alone to take.

The only law is Love, and love will guide you in whatever choices you must make.

Certainty

Like a suit of shining armour,
Polished gold that gleams and sparkles in the light.
That 'Blessed Shield' that keeps our ego safe.
No nagging doubts disturb us in the night.
No second thoughts to make our conscience chafe.

The Joy of never being wrong,
Those great eternal truths that beam down from above.
Our principles that keep us different from the milling throng.
When we love Certainty,
Its charms can keep us safe from any other love.

We feel misunderstood by those who do not truly 'Know'.
Their dreadful ignorance and anarchy surround us every day.
If only we could set them on the path they need to go, -
If only they could understand the things we try to say,
Then we could let them bask in our enlightened glow.

But then, I paused and wondered at the world.
Who was it taught the sparrow how to fly?
They always seemed to know just what to do,
Before I ever had a chance to teach them how.
And sang their joyous songs of courtship, long before I told them to.

I often watch in envy as they dance and weave beneath the evening sky.
The crimson setting sun, that lights their antics, lights the

furrows on my brow.

Streaking red and gold across the purple hills and dark green fields,

It's rainbow glory blinds my world-worn eyes and lets my spirit see,

This world was doing fine before there ever was a me.

Quantum Physics for Dummies

I looked on Amazon today for something new to read,
Something to inform my brain, and help in times of need.
I thought I'd take it easy, and start with something small.
Quantum physics seemed quite perfect for a chap like me – who isn't very tall.

I read the introduction and I felt quite optimistic at the start…
"A book that anyone can understand" – well this bit warmed my heart!
But when I read the 'ifs' and 'buts', - my ardour hit a downward slope.
It seems I need to master higher math's to make it as a dope!

If you've read Aesop's fables, you will understand why suddenly these grapes seemed rather sour.
A simple failing – like the absence of a math's degree had robbed me of my finest hour.
I could have understood the secrets of the Cosmos, like some medieval mage.
Pontificating on the mysteries of a world that had become my star-lit stage.

Now, I'll have to stick to poetry – the type that rhymes and never makes a cent.
And I'll sit back in my dotage wondering where my chance for fame and fortune went.
If only I had stayed in school an extra year, or two, or three, or

even four?

The world and all its riches might have beat a pathway to my peerless door.

Pathways in Time.

I stand amazed and ask myself how can this really be?

If I have walked this street a thousand years ago, then who, exactly can I be?

Strange memories engulf my mind of someone who I don't recall as me.

In this short life I've walked this street a hundred times and never saw the things which I now see.

The shimmering path seems almost physical where town and forest merge.

Yet others wander past, without awareness of the glowing point where paths converge.

The cobbled footpath wanders on past shops and tidy houses, - nestled all along the narrow lane.

And yet, for me the path winds slowly upwards to a land I thought I'd never see again.

Oh! Sweet Ireland, how I've longed to see your forests and your waters once again.

But now, I feel that when I walked your roads before, I was not of the race of men.

The trees seemed so much taller and each hedgerow gave sufficient shelter for a creature of my kind.

And now, I walk the hidden path again and leave this world behind.

The cobblestones have slipped away and I can hear a whisper in the trees.

I hear the rustle of the leaves upon the forest floor as ferns are brushing past my knees.

I have scarcely walked a dozen steps and yet the town seems very far away.

An ancient peace descends upon me as I wander down an old familiar trail I've never walked before today.

I wonder if I'm going home at last to that beloved land where none grow tired or old.

That place where ancient songs are sung and timeless stories told.

That land where every kettle's full and every crock is filled with gleaming gold.

A place where every bard feels welcome, and the ancient stories are retold.

I journeyed westward, - 'til I came to Galway's rugged shores.

There beside her barren rocks, the coracle was tied, - just as it was in dreams I had before.

Led along by four white swans, I travelled swiftly homeward to the western isles.

Where I was welcomed by my long-lost kin with many hugs and smiles.

Although the feasting and the drinking may go on for many, many years.

And there will be so many songs of joy, and many happy tears.

I'll keep a touch of warmth within my heart for all the friends I'll never see again.

But now that I am home, - I know that I will never walk again upon the world of men.

On Saying Goodbye.

Please don't wait until you're leaving me to give me one last kiss goodbye.
I feel your heartbeat drifting far away with every mournful, soulful sigh.
I know it's raining, but let's grab our coats and walk along some mud-soaked country lane.
I have this dreadful feeling that the fleeting moments we have left may never come again.

I have said goodbye too many times to people who I never got to speak to any more.
And now I understand how brutally the cards may fall when fate comes knocking at our door.
The careless wave, each time we say farewell – the little stories that we never get to share,
The times we should have hugged, but never did, become the burdens that we cannot bear.

So, learn to choose your friends and enemies with both perceptiveness and care.
And when you play the game of life, to really live your part, you must be brave and fair.
The people who adorn your life will always be much greater than the pallid roles that you can see.
Each one of us contains a universe of dreams and hopes for all the things that we may never be.

To everyone that I have loved, I wish that I had learned to love you so much more.

It's tragic that it takes so long to learn that learning how to love is really what our life is for.

When finally, we learn that most important lesson, it is often time to learn to say goodbye.

And still the most important words we have to say are hidden with a mournful, soulful sigh.

CHAPTER 8: MOONSTRUCK IN DUBLIN.

Walking down the shimmering streets,
With neon lights reflecting as I gaze down at my feet.
The recent rain did little to subdue the passer-bye's delight.
As I walk through Dublin City, on a moonlit summer's night.

Lover's walking hands in hand and laughter in the wind.
A city's heart that beats with love – but love won't let me in.
I cannot share their happiness tonight, perhaps I never will again.
Tonight, I lost my only love, my angel and my one and only friend.

In my defence, I only wanted you to love me.
From the moment we first met, I ached to see you free.
I believed I only ever longed to heal your broken wings.
And in my foolish heart, I thought that this was how our life should be.

I thought you recognised me as the one who held your heart.
I thought I held it gently in my hands, and we would never be apart.
But as your wounded wings grew strong, you tried to fly away.
I grasped too tight and left you with a wounded heart, the day you flew away.

I tried hard to believe that we could still be friends to fill my empty hands.

Those hands that longed to hold you close could never understand.

The love that needs too much can never be a love that lasts.

And even hungry hands can never grasp enough to hold on to what's past.

I sit here by the Liffey as the streets grow quiet and cool.

I wonder at how easily we play at being the fool.

I almost had a love that might have been forever, but my heart was needy and my grip was much too tight.

I gaze across the moonlit water, knowing that my sins may wash away before the ending of the night.

Beyond the Ragged Fields

Beyond the ragged, rocky fields and crumbling dry-stone walls, we walked, - as lovers often do.

Her drunken father slept, as quietly beyond his beggared boundaries we crept.

Beneath her long black dress, her snow-white feet were bathed by the morning dew.

Her beauty was divine, and though her tender heart was mine,

The innocence beneath her long black dress, no love had ever known.

Ah! Sweet Eileen, I would die for just one kiss from your sweet lips.

No rouge has ever stained the softness which my eyes alone have managed to caress.

I cannot win your father's grace with gifts or land or gold,

For fortune has not shone upon this travelling man, - though I am brave and bold.

I have fought in many wars but now my horse and gun have long been sold.

If I could find Fitzgibbon, - he's a colonel in the army and one day I saved his life.

I am sure his gratitude would set me up so I could ask for you to be my wife.

But he is many miles away and long before I could return, I fear that you'll be wed.

And I would pluck the eyes from my own head before I'd see you in another's bed.

Although I've lived through many wars, without you by my side
I may as well be dead.

Come with me across the sea to where a man and woman can
live free.
There are lands and plenty for the brave who dare to risk the
tempests and the waves.
I'll take the shilling one more time if you will promise to be
mine.
And then, our passage will be paid to find our fortune far across
the sea.
Where we can start a family and build a bright new life for you
and me.

Her soft, brown eyes were all that gave reply as on they walked
beneath a misty sky.
She slipped her hand in his as morning mist became a blanket of
the softest weave.
Stepping blindly forward, they embraced their brave new world,
While all around, the thick white morning fog began to whirl.
And in the little village, all were woken by the ringing of a single
bell.

A kindly neighbour saw them walking in the early morning fog,
And shook his head at youthful folly, as they wandered hand in
hand into the bog.
I hope they found their brave new world, - for they were never
seen again since that sad day.
No letter ever came from far away, and not a single word for fifty
years.

And every time that church bell rang her father drank a little more to hide his bitter tears.

The Ancient Queen

She loved the smell of rain on summer nights.
Weaving through the web of dreams that brought the dreamers
terror and delight.
Above the glistening streets that glittered past beneath her
moonlit flight.
She looked just like a sleepless dragonfly to those who lacked the
clarity of sight.

Almost underneath the trees and almost underneath the cities'
garish lights,
Almost on the roofs of barns and houses – almost solid where
she would alight.
Her dreamers toss and turn and almost wake each time she
touched their souls.
Some hearts would never be the same. Some never would grow
old.

She sang of ancient forests and of ancient memories each time
she flew.
The songs she sang were older than the mountains, - newer than
the morning dew.
Singing in an ancient language that the sons of men had never
understood,
She sang of feasts and dancing underneath the endless woods.

Once upon a time her home was more than dreams, and spread
from shore to shore.
Long before the sons of man had cut and burned her trees and

smelted iron ore.

The spirits of her children trapped within the cursed metal by the searing fires.

As the ancient forests fell to man's unquenchable desire.

Now her children sleep in peace beneath the earth where no man dares to till.

In the remnants of the woodlands and the ancient sacred hills.

Even in his folly, man had learned to leave their resting place alone.

For who could save the man for whom she judged a sin must be atoned?

More Lives Than One?

They say that there are many, many, other worlds, and yet,
This world that I have learned to love has many joys and pleasures all its own.
Since I was five years old, I chased those other worlds,
And now, I realise another sixty precious years have flown.

I don't regret the many thousand books I read,
When, every night, I lay, unsleeping in my bed.
Nor hiding in my secret places less I should be sought and found
–
Disturbed from all my wistful thoughts of other worlds where mysteries abound.

So many other worlds were mine, but maybe they were worlds I found too soon?
This world that I rejected was the world the Universe had given as a gift to me.
I took it all too seriously and never took the time to play the fool or act the 'loon'.
And now it seems that laughter, fun and climbing trees was all that life was ever meant to be.

Wisdom comes to everyone, and life, - with all its grit, is all it takes to polish up our souls.
Life is just a game and all we have to do is play our allocated roles.
Having fun is not a crime and nothing's lost for those who dance through life.
Sometimes we have to face it, but our lives were never planned to

be an endless wheel of pain and strife.

Teach your children how to laugh and sing and show them love and all the benefits it brings.
There are no monsters in the sky, and Life, Herself, will pick them up each time they fall.
The heaven that we seek lies safe within our hearts, we hear it every time a sparrow sings.
There are no sacrifices that we need to make. The Universe will hold us safely in Her hands, - if we would only call.

Once Upon a Time

Once upon a time we were like sparks up in the air.

Floating high above the flame like faeries – living life without a care.

Once upon a time we flew like birds, high in the sky,

Never having ever wondered, Who? or, Where? or, Why?

Once upon a time we floated, just like fish do, – in the sea.

I doubt we ever pondered on the 'me' that we would be?

In the dappled light and muffled sounds, we heard the music of our future world,

But if I asked you if we worried about life? You'd think I was absurd.

Once upon a time we realised that we inherited a name.

A useful label to describe the people we became.

But somehow, we became convinced the games we played were real.

We lost control of how we saw the world and how we really feel.

What if learning how to steal is just another way of learning how to give?

What if learning how to hate, is just a way to learn how to forgive.

In our darkest sins we find for certain what can never bring us light.

From our deepest pain and sorrow come the seeds that someday bring delight.

Perhaps you have a cruel god who punishes a sinful world?

Perhaps you have a Goddess who delights in dance and smiles at every whirl?

Perhaps the beating of your drum inspires your heart to beat with love?

Perhaps your life is guided by the angels or the other beings who fly so far above?

Perhaps your life consists of many other things of which I have no time to speak?

Perhaps you choose to live without a god, but still defend the poor and weak?

I wish you well in every universe we share each time your world collides with mine.

I want to share a secret that is hidden deep in every world,

Your world will work out fine.

Pontification

They say I am dense, with a view so intense,
That nothing disturbs my convictions.
Not science nor religion, nor even that pigeon,
That just had a poo on my scientific fictions.

I work in my garden to get some fresh air.
But now there's a mess on my keys.
Oh! Wait! When I wiped them, it almost made sense!
Strange words – but I'll sound quite impressive with these!

The light can't get in and the sound bounces off.
My bubble is perfectly sound.
I know I'm a genius, and I'm always right.
I'm the cleverest person around.

I've not heard an argument proving me wrong.
Since I was evicted from school,
For wrecking the class when they failed me at maths,
And for calling the teacher a fool.

Some say I'm big-headed, but I know they're wrong.
My hat size is only a ten.
So, I went back to school, just to prove I'm no fool,
But the buggers just won't let me in!

Do Not Tell Me Death is Nothing

Do not tell me death is nothing. Death is truly half of life.

It is not just the end of someone's sorrow, pain or strife.

For those of us who wait behind, the pain is much too hard to bear.

While in the quietest darkest corners of our minds we wonder, "What is there?"

I have spoken to the dead, and yet, I do not know what I will find...

They do not seem to care about the place of their repose – they speak about the world they left behind.

And as for me, the pain of losing those I love may never truly heal.

There is never proof enough to comfort me or change the way I feel.

This world may be more solid, but less real, than all the worlds which lie ahead.

The only problem is we only get to know for sure when we are also dead.

When I was young, I would have traded life to find that place where truth and freedom lies,

But now, I'm old and I can see that truth is here before our very eyes.

Life and Death are lovers locked in an eternal dance.

This world is just the table where we cast our dice and take another chance.

It is only right that we should rage and cry for what we've loved and lost,
Then live our fullest life and be our greatest selves - whatever it may cost,

We do not know for certain, what may lie beyond that great divide,
So, why not walk this world in kindness so we pass in peace onto that other side?
Death was never nothing. Death has waited patiently since we were born.
But when we pass away, Is Life not waiting also – like the dawn of a new morn?

Would It Be So Sad?

Would it be so sad if I could never reach the moon?
Is it such a tragedy that I have never held a silver spoon?
Is my life a waste because my life is so mundane?
And if my many, long forgotten wishes were fulfilled,
would I still feel the very same?

All of it is almost past and gone, as you and I both know -
The rain, the sunny days, the frosty mornings and the drifting snow.
Life has trickled through my fingers like a careless hand,
Lying on the beach and clutching warm dry sand,
Imagination spins away, creating distant lands.

But do these lands exist beyond the machinations of my mind?
If I slowly breathe and look inside my own imagination - what exactly, will I find?
The memories are just as real as any moment in my life.
The world and all its mysteries exist inside of me, -
The beauty and the sorrow, the kindness and the strife.

It is not too late to change this world of wonder that I've made.
But it fits me like a glove, I am the orchestrator of my own parade.
They say 'Acceptance' is the key, and I accept the good and bad that I have done.
The victories, the joys, the trepidations and the fun.
And anyway, who knows what's next?
My race is not yet run.

PATRICKWILLIAMKAVANAGH

Colours

Wild eyed prophets dressed in garish, multi-coloured robes.

Born with visions of the star, the cross, the crescent and the goddess as she rose.

Fringes on the garment of society and waving softly in the wind.

But who will keep the cold away when winter's storms roll in?

Dressed for summer days and summer nights of gentle dreams.

Writing, singing, talking of the world you dreamed and what it means.

Living lovingly within an empty world where empty pockets are a crime.

Reaching out with love and hoping that your love will somehow be returned sometime.

The rainbow colours of your life reflect the rainbow colours of your hearts.

Leaving all the pain and all the hurt behind to try to make another start.

Finding friends who shared your vision, and your dreams, became your only need,

In this world where tanks and missiles serve the makers of your brother's greed.

I should have held your hand and left this world of slavery and subterfuge behind,

But I was ill-prepared to take that load and walk that road and see what I might find.

I was bound and blinded by the rules, and thought you

vagabonds and fools,
But now I see a world beyond this world where only love and
vibrant colours rule.

We Are Going to Be Alright

We are going to be alright.

I know you sometimes hear the children crying in the night.

I know you hold your breath and listen carefully in fright.

We think we hear whatever ghosts we fear are scratching at our door.

But soon enough, we'll find ourselves in that sweet place where we were, once before.

And as we glide serenely into that eternity of light,

We'll realise that everything is going to be alright.

We are going to be alright.

Look out the window at the moon when she is shining bright.

Remember Her when stormy clouds obscure Her guiding light.

I know the world can be a scary place when we have slipped away from grace,

The world seems lonely and we long for one familiar face.

But when we let our lonely hearts reach out into the sacred night,

We touch the Universe and realise that we will be alright.

We are going to be alright.

The Winter's fading fast and Spring will soon festoon the lanes with garlands of delight,

A promise of the summer days to come when roses bloom and dragonflies alight.

When butterflies go fluttering by and falcons hover in the clear, blue sky,

And even if we're miles apart, I'll reach out to your loving heart,

and sigh,
And when I feel you reaching back, I'll know the reason why,
I feel that everything is going to be alright.

Broken Love

One day the truth will shine,
That evil men have filled our minds with fearful lies and drink
our fear like finest wine.
They whisper twisted truths into our ears, and sisters call their
sisters liars.
They raise the crescent and the cross until the night is lit with
fires.
Burning buildings all around and foolish brothers screaming in
the smoke-filled air.
I search the charred and broken streets for love, but only broken
love is there.

It seems like wars may never end.
The children that they put in uniforms are not yet old enough to
bend.
Everything to them is simply black and white,
For in the childish mind there's only wrong and right.
Fuelled by ignorance and led by foolish pride,
The young are always ready for the fight.

From the shelter of their bunkers,
Rich old men with skin like parchment rub their hands in glee.
War is good for business, but their jaded appetites cannot be
quenched with gold,
Their wrinkled hands with jewelled claws are reaching out for
you and me
Mankind is the only prey that's left, - with all of nature's bounty
fallen to their greed.

Poisoned hearts, corrupting all they touch, who blight the earth with poisoned seed.

One day, the truth will shine because one day it must.

When the world has learned to love, the world of greed will crumble into dust.

Smile by smile, we build a future that is kind, and kindness never kills.

Hug by hug we'll raise our children to be kind and live by strength of will.

When their only certainty is that we love them, they can face the world with open eyes.

With unbroken hearts, our children can create a world of love and not a world of lies.

Chapter 9: Down The Garden Path

Down the winding gravel path, where pebbles gleam with rainbow hues,
Underneath the trellised arch and through the little wooden door,
There, where rich red roses bloom and almost touch the floor.
I found a land, that I am sure, was never there before.

The golden sun that gently lit the sky above, was smiling at a sleepy turtle dove,
Who'd realised he'd slept too late, and now with drowsy eyes was searching for his mate.
The busy bees were bumbling by, and bumping into butterflies, who slowly fluttered by.
And by a river where the salmon leapt, I heard the willows sigh.

A heady fragrance filled the air and made my senses swim, - then I became aware,
that somehow as I rambled through this wonderland, a mouse had nested in my hair.
"Good morning, Mrs Mouse", said I. She peered between my eyebrows, looking rather shy.
"I can't pay any rent", she said, then scurried back onto my head, and never said goodbye.

Unperturbed, I walked down to the river just to sit and watch the swans.

Alabaster sails that caught the morning wind, and in a moment, they were gone.

Then as I watched the faeries dance, I fell into my normal, busy, day-time trance,

And all the magic disappeared before my blinkered glance.

The Path of Dreams

Perhaps our dreams can never change the world in just a day.
Maybe we were made to simply be the evening star that points the way.
The crazy ones, the lazy ones, the ones who can't be swayed.
We walk and talk and dress as if the world was a parade.

We were never meant for beige or grey, or clothes of sombre hue,
Although the purity of black on white – at least for some of us - will do.
When we rest, we rest in silence and in darkness until our sorrow fades away.
When we rise, we rise in gratitude to face another bright new day.

Do not think us shallow or unkind because we will not live in fear.
Do not think we do not grieve when we have lost what we hold dear.
We smile with hope and swathe our sorrows in a shroud of love to keep us warm.
We see and love a universe which holds us in its palm and does not mean us harm.

On Being Human

If my words can calm your fears, or even dry your tears, then all my work is not in vain.

If all my words can't dry your tears, I'll close the book on all my wasted years and never write again.

Sometimes, I feel I understand your pain, and, in those times, I feel that you see mine.

And if my words don't touch your heart, please understand that caring was my only crime.

I need to tell you – even in your solitude and sorrow - you are seen and known.

I need to know that you know, you are loved, and have no need to ever feel alone.

You may wonder why I even care, or you may ask yourself just what it is I hope to gain?

But I am just a fleeting shadow passing by and I may never pass this way again.

We are born from dirt and stardust. Spirits bursting from the earth like every flower and tree.

In our flesh and blood and bones we carry every form of earthly life that there can ever be.

When we look into our soul we see the wolf, the bear, the antelope, and every creature of the sea.

In our flawed imperfect selves, we hold the secrets of the Universe, that one day, all will see.

In the Olden Days

In the olden days the young men went to war with shiny buttons on their coats.

In their pocket was a shiny shilling for the lives they gave away with ill-considered oaths.

Fresh-faced children filled with lies of monsters who existed underneath a different sky.

They charged the cannons, and they threw away their youth and never knew the reason why.

We had empires then whose leaders dressed in gold and who were proud to show their wealth.

Kings and emperors who were unashamed of all their evil acts and never cared for stealth.

The peasants lined the streets and cheered to see their blood and toil, in purple silk displayed.

Dirty and unkempt, not one of them could understand, what kind of deal their distant ancestors had made.

In that distant time when mankind first decided they could own the rivers and the land.

The serpents came and built the walls that barred us from the promised land.

Paradise was lost. That former earth where every woman and her children wandered free.

Behind the sweat-and-blood-stained walls, mankind was forced to find another way to be.

Now the wars we fight no longer leave our heroes bodies

scattered on a no-mans-land.

War has stepped into our homes and in the city streets where children battle hand-to-hand.

No longer fed our lies by pamphlets we can see our crimes in living colour on our HD, TV screens.

We shake our heads while people cheer their masters and they still don't understand exactly what it means.

On Visiting the Gentle Folk.

I love to sit and talk with you, but part of me is calling me away.
A little place within my soul is longing for the Fae.
A place that's filled with summer's flowers and birds that sing such joyful songs,
That just a little part of me is yearning for the place where I belong.

I love to keep you company. My heart rejoices with your every smile.
The beauty that you hide behind your mask makes every day worthwhile.
Your laughter lifts my spirits, and your giggles lighten up my day,
But still a tiny, tiny part of me is called to somewhere far away.

And if I go, I know it may not be for just a little while.
And who can say for certain if I can return once more in time to see you smile?
This land of time is fleeting, and, in the other-world, a day may last a hundred years.
I dare not risk a journey that may bring me back some day to see your children's tears.

Beauty

Never lose your beauty, -
never mind the scars that life inevitably brings.
Keep the freshness in your heart of Bluebells
that delight the woodland roads in spring.

Life may bring a bitter taste,
But bitterness was never yours to keep.
Keep the sweetness of a princess,
In her poisoned sleep.

Unlike the fairy tales, you do not need
a knight in shining armour to release your soul.
You are Woman – Fountain of all life.
The world was always yours to hold.

The beauty in your heart can raise a generation
Who are born to raise the light of love up high.
The wisdom of your life can teach your children's children
How to reach beyond the skies.

Faery Dreams and Memories

It is easy to survive with all your questions buried by the busyness of trying to stay alive.
But when we reach a resting place, our thoughts are soon to stray.
We wonder at the chance that somewhere in our struggle to survive.
We somehow lost the wisdom and the wit to truly thrive.

I miss the gentle Fae. I wonder if they truly went away.
Or were the busy streets too full of lights and noise.
And was I blinded by my challenges, and somehow lost that poise,
That let me see those gentle folk at play.

Where we once had wolves to sing Her praise, the wind is howling at the Moon.
That blessed sister that we share will glide across the heavens much too soon.
It breaks my heart to see Her shining through the stark and naked trees.
Remembering the times, she filled the night with gentle light for you and me.

Soon the busy times will pass, and I will search for you in valleys, hills and glens.
My heart assures me that some summer evening by some tiny brook – we'll meet again.

Until that time has come, I'll soothe my aching heart with memories I've cherished for so long,

Of when we danced along the dusty roads and sang our wild, free songs.

Act 1 Scene 2

There is a light which casts no shadow and a darkness which illuminates our world.
In their warp and weave a tapestry is woven where our stories can be told.
Light and darkness intertwine as figures dance across the stage.
The music of our beating hearts provides the rhythm as our song is played.

I remember long ago when I was told this world was just a stage.
You can't believe that when you're young – there are so many parts you've not yet played.
We see the world as tragedy or comedy; a bold adventure or a chance to shine.
And though our words reveal our lives as play – the realisation takes a little time.

The curtain's not yet lowered and still the spotlight shines upon the stage.
The leading actors sing about their love or bellow out their rage.
The audience are so enraptured that they never want to see it's all 'pretend'.
Who knows what twists the plot will take before the scene has reached it end?

Tears and Laughter

Like a river, tears have flowed through every lane and every pasture of my life.
I guess that every meadow needs the rain, and not all tears are tears of pain.
But still, I never laughed enough at all the tragicomedies that made my life.
I focused too much on the pain and now I realise those years will never come again.

I dare not ask the gods for laughter – lest they take my fragile sanity away.
I think we need to start the habit early in our lives when we are learning how to play.
They told me that the world was just a battleground, and I was born to fight.
It took too many years to learn; - this world was made for laughter and delight.

But I have breath within me yet for laughter, and I have wit and sight enough to see.
Though bones may ache, and knees may quake – there's joy enough in life for folk like me.
We have won and lost so many battles – we have passed and failed so many tests.
The time that we have left is better spent in laughter as we meander gently towards our rest.

Rory MacDowell and the Unseelie Queen

Many a man has been led from the path and has earned his reward of an unending wrath.

But none were so foolish as Rory MacDowell, a once kind young man who turned irksome and foul.

With a fine pair of brogues and a spine like a rod, none could match Rory at lifting a hod.

He worked like a mule, and he drank like a hog, and Rory feared nothing – not faerie nor God.

He sang like an angel – you'd hear him each night. The girls in the pub would all scream with delight.

And Rory was handsome - a manly delight, a morsel to cause the young ladies to fight

His life was a battle, a party, a ball - but sooner or later the prideful must fall.

His prowess was known to both one and to all, and his fame lured the Queen of the Dark Fae to call.

Mab was a weaver of wonderful dreams, she tempted with pleasures and wonderful scenes.

The sleeper would waken with fevers and sweats, from dreams that could only be cured by their deaths.

The longings they felt – they could never assuage. In time all their love turned to anger and rage.

Though their journey had started with laughter and feasts, as their sanity faded, they turned into beasts.

Well, Rory met Mab on a cold winter's eve, and she wove him a web of desire and intrigue.

She melted his heart with her cold careless kiss, and she led him away with a promise of bliss.

Each night she would take him - each day he'd return and all through the day Rory's longing would burn.

He grew harsh and bitter, - he drank through the day, until health and good looks had all faded away.

When his beauty had faded and his waist had grown stout, the Unseelie Queen had grown tired of the lout.

She soon found another, of that there's no doubt. She reviled poor old Rory and then cast him out.

He awoke sometime later; we don't know just when. He was found in a barn with the hay and the hens.

His wits had long fled him, he cried like a child, and the eyes in his head were both frenzied and wild.

If My Words

If my words can make you smile, then walk with me along the quiet lanes.

Those leafy walks where kindly spirits fill our minds with peaceful reveries.

Perhaps there'll be a rainbow as the rain clouds drift away.

That multi-coloured promise from the sun that there will always be a better day.

If my words have made you sad, then let us walk beside a lonely pool.

The tears I offer you are never harvested from irreparable despair.

The tears we shed are tears of healing – washing all our pain away.

Those tears that wash away the past and bring a bright new day.

If my words seem less than real, remember that we share the things we really feel.

Reaching out with heart and mind, is how we realise our bond is real.

The world we share is truer the world that we find everywhere.

That world where we imagine all we see is all the world was ever meant to be.

If my words can make your world complete, then take my hand and walk with me.

If my words can resonate with yours, then let us make our world become the best that it can be.

If our worlds can resonate with others who can see a better world for all.

Then we can take each other's hand until that world is built – lest we should fall

When You Love

When you love, remember you must never count the cost.
If you count your love like miser's pennies, then your love's already lost.
Measured love means nothing – all you count as gain is loss.
When you love, it must be everything – a partial love is dross.

When you love, remember not to bind your love with rules.
Love is not a contract for a lifetime of contentment or of bliss.
All who truly love must leap, and all true lovers must be fools.
Their higher wisdom risks the promises within a lover's kiss.

Never listen to the thieves who try to steal your love away.
Love was never made for cowards. Love will always bring us pain.
Fearful hearts who sacrificed their love for comfort slowly fade away.
And although each love must end, a heart that's filled with love will always love again.

Star Gazing.

Deep within the forest,
Far beyond the sea,
High above the mountains,
Where my heart is free.

Breathing deeply, as I feel the earth beneath my feet.
Sighing softly as my tension slips away.
I remember that my mother's touch is everywhere.
And every path I take will take me on my rightful way.

Even on the city streets, I feel the beat of angel's wings.
Tiny Faeries flutter all around and make me smile.
Despite the roar of passing traffic, I can hear them softly sing.
The many guides and messengers whose love became their only
toil.

We who walk this world as flesh and can't remember who we
are.
We are not alone, and all our pain and joy will never go unseen.
As daylight fades and naked twilight sets a backdrop for the
stars.
I gaze out at the beauty all around and I remember all I've been.

On Being Whole

I stand alone, yet in the middle of a joyous, chanting crowd.

Their chosen word for God reverberates from heart to heart and wall to sacred wall.

Although they sing out their devotion with a voice so clear and loud.

I feel as isolated as another might, if there was no one here at all.

I who worship nothing, feel more lost than I have ever felt before.

I envy them their idols and their certainty, that long ago I might have shared.

Sometimes I wish that I could reignite the childish faith I had before,

When I believed there was a kind and loving Deity who held me in their care.

But I have Nothingness to free my mind and kindness soothes my soul.

The Great Abyss awaits when all the troubles and the pain become too great.

Bathing in the Dark where all our shattered fragments fuse into a greater whole.

Until my heart returns me, once again, to face whatever years are left to wait.

When Our Wings Unfold.

When our wings unfold, our minds will fly above illusion's sway.
We will see the sun that always shines above the darkest clouds.
Gazing down with joy upon a world that suddenly seems bright and gay,
We will laugh to see how foolishly we once believed that we had lost our way.

Before we learned the words that shaped our thoughts and minds,
We had the memories of all the worlds that we had left behind.
Irritated though we were by childish appetites and needs.
We remembered for a little while that we were Nature's seed.

The tiny bodies that our spirits blessed were full of appetites and fears.
Long forgotten monsters from the dawn of Mankind's years.
Flesh and spirit moulded into history, responsibility and Fate.
Many of us only learned just who we were when it was just too late.

We saw the dawning of a brand-new life just as we left this life behind.
We smiled at all the fears and tears which filled the life that we had left behind.
As our spirits soared into a land of joy and endless sun.
We thanked the Universe for everything that we had lost,
And everything that we had won.

LEAVES

A million stories blow across the forest of my mind,
Like the fallen leaves that Autumn winds have gently left behind.
They lay in scattered piles in the embrace of winters naked trees.
So many little nests of warmth against the Winter's breeze.

They are my friends; each little leaf that holds a story wrapped within its brittle folds.
A million stories resting underneath the trees until their tale is told.
I lay among the whispering leaves and listen to them all the winter long.
Grateful that when Springtime comes, the world will sing a million brand-new songs.

They are not mine – these stories that I borrow from the trees.
They are a gift from Mother, sent to give you comfort and a sense of ease.
A million stories gathered by the wind as Autumn brings the world to rest.
The wisdom of the forest sent to bring your soul to rest.

Their words are simple, and their rhythm taken from the heartbeat of the earth.
Their wisdom grows within like seeds upon the sacred forest dirt.
They speak to me of peace for peace is all the forest knows.
They speak to me of kindness as they lead me down the paths

where I must go.

THE WIND

The wind was like a different form of silence,
As she whispered through the trees.
She fluttered like a moth around my mind.
And brought a sense of rest and ease
In the darkness, she caressed me like an old familiar friend.
When my time of hope and doubt had finally reached its end

Do not mourn for me when I am gone.
Let my memory lie softly on your mind
and soothe you like a favourite childhood song.
Love can bear all losses - love can heal all pain.
Love can keep me safely in your heart
'Til I return again.

In the bosom of the wind was where my heart flew free.
I followed her wherever she would lead, to find another way to be.
Perhaps the wind will change and she will bring me back again?
But if she does, I cannot tell you how or where or when.
For I have placed my soul within her tender care
And so, I say goodbye for now, my friend.

ABOUT THE AUTHOR

Patrick W Kavanagh

Patrick's mother was a psychic who read playing cards and tea leaves and he learned to read Tarot cards from an early age. He continued to give readings throughout his life as time allowed, often at charity events and sometimes working for online websites.

Patrick was fascinated by the link between mental health, spirituality, and expressing subconscious needs through both divination and creative writing.

Patrick and his wife, Tina who is a spiritual medium, spent many years conducting demonstrations of mediumship, clairvoyance and drumming therapy in the United Kingdom.

Finally settled in Dublin, Patrick returned to education and took courses in Community health and social studies and is now completing a creative writing course at Maynooth University.

He is training to become a creative writing facilitator to help others to gain the resilience that he feels writing has given him. Patrick has published books on poetry, mysticism, grief and Fairy folklore.

BOOKS BY THIS AUTHOR

When Tears Will Not Come

I wote these poems after the passing of my late wife, Frances. The act of writing and sharing them brought acceptance and healing, both to myself and others.I believe that Carl Jung was right about the existence of a 'collective unconscious'. I found that reaching inwards and writing or journalling can put us in touch with a wisdom that we may never have suspected to exist.

King Of The Faeries

This is a collection of poems devoted to fairy folklore and contains many stories in rhyme that are suitable for all ages. Some are funny; some are scary, but all of them are with the intention of bringing the world of our imagination to life.

Faery Fact And Fairy Fiction

This books examines the fairy faith and it includes sightings, folklore, meditations and artwork by the graphic artist, Bill Oliver. There is also a print-only version available, due to the high cost of colour print for this version of the book.

Finding Your Own Way

Personal Meditations for Mastery and Self-knowledge.This is essential reading for those with an interest in the occult or spirituality. No-nonsense advice on the basics of Magic and Meditation is combined with beautiful and inspiring prose and art to facilitate successful meditation and spiritual development.

Winds Of Change: Poetry Of Compassion

'Winds of Change' is a poet's view of the fringes of society. Tramps and beggars vie with the privileged and powerful to entice us into sharing their experiences. In stories spanning the past, present, and future, almost mythical characters leap from the pages to remind us of those brief moments when the world seemed to have more purpose and possibilities than we normally imagine.

Teddy Bard's Tales

Teddy Bard is very much like us. He has faced loss and grief, victory and defeat. He has struggled and fallen many times, - only to drag himself back onto his feet and carry on. Somehow, by surviving for over sixty years, Teddy has accumulated a fund of wit and wisdom which he wishes to share with the world. There will be laughter and tears, - smiles and chills, and possibly, a new way of seeing the world which may free us from past suffering. I guarantee that you will find this collection of stories in verse to be both entertaining and insightful.

A WORD OF THANKS
TO MY READERS

Thank you to everyone who has supported me over the years. I believe that everyone needs and deserves to be heard. It is essential to what makes us human. I hope that the thoughts and reflections in my books brought comfort and inspiration.

May your future be bright, and filled with kindness and compassion.

Patrick W Kavanagh
09/04/2024

Printed in Great Britain
by Amazon